FULL ON EMPTY

THE SPIRITUAL EXPERIENCE OF A FORTY DAY FAST

KELLY CARROLL

TATE PUBLISHING & Enterprises

This book is designed to provide accurate and authoritative information with regard to the subject matter covered. This information is given with the understanding that neither the author nor Tate Publishing, LLC is engaged in rendering legal, professional advice. Since the details of your situation are fact dependent, you should additionally seek the services of a competent professional.

The opinions expressed by the author are not necessarily those of Tate Publishing, LLC.

Published by Tate Publishing & Enterprises, LLC
127 E. Trade Center Terrace | Mustang, Oklahoma 73064 USA
1.888.361.9473 | www.tatepublishing.com

Tate Publishing is committed to excellence in the publishing industry. The company reflects the philosophy established by the founders, based on Psalm 68:11,
"The Lord gave the word and great was the company of those who published it."

Book design copyright © 2011 by Tate Publishing, LLC. All rights reserved.
Cover design by Blake Brasor
Interior design by Nathan Harmony

Published in the United States of America

ISBN: 978-1-61777-336-5
1. Religion / Christian Life / General
2. Religion / Christian Life / Personal Growth
11.04.21

FULL ON
EMPTY

Dedication

This book is dedicated to Jesus Christ, lover of my life, Savior of my soul, the light of the world!

I thank you, Lord, for redeeming me from the pit of hell and from the clutches of the evil one. Your mercy and grace surround me like a shield, and your presence in my life is my refuge.

I dedicate my life to you, Jesus, with a thankful heart. You provide all things for me, and your love has restored my life and made all things new again.

Your forgiveness and grace will continue to follow me and my entire family. Your blessings are the promises you have given me through faith. Your love for me is my true inheritance.

Praise you, heavenly Father, for the glory you shine down on this earth. My prayer is that your will be done on earth as it is in heaven.

Acknowledgments

For the love of you: my heart goes out in prayer for blessings and renewal, for love and for eternal life…

Travis and Tara Fisher and beautiful Maya, my first granddaughter, I love you with all my heart and soul.

Carlos, Heidi, and Andy and my lovely Natalyah, who is my second granddaughter of joy and blessings from above.

Mom (who is with Jesus now) and my dad, who taught me to never give up and, no matter what happens in this life, to have mercy and loving forgiveness for family, because we only have one earthly family given to us by God.

To my older siblings, Craig, Maryann, Diana, and Nita… my most treasured sister who has always had my back.

To my sweet dear friend Margie Munter Ginsberg, a beloved friend God placed in my life for a divine purpose and perfect timing.

To Susan Johnson my dear friend in Christ.

To Glynis Warner a deep and caring soul who watched my back in college and is still here with me today.

To Jackie Delgado my sister in Christ that has taught me the importance of being like-minded and a healthy temple for Christ.

May the God of Jesus Christ overtake you with love, healing, long life, and his mercy following you all the days of your life.

The Lord gives the command;

> The women who proclaim the good tidings are a great host
>
> Psalm 68:11 (NASB)
>
> The Lord gave the word: great was the company of those that published it.
>
> Psalm 68:11 (KJV)

> This is the message we have heard from him and declare to you: God is light; in him there is no darkness at all. If we claim to have fellowship with him yet walk in the darkness, we lie and do not live by the truth. But if we walk in the light, as he is in the light, we have fellowship with one another, and the blood of Jesus, his Son, purifies us from all sin. If we claim to be without sin, we deceive ourselves and the truth is not in us. If we confess our sins, he is faithful and just and will forgive us our sins and purify us from all unrighteousness. If we claim we have not sinned, we make him out to be a liar and his word has no place in our lives.
>
> 1 John 1:5–10 (NIV)

He loves you, and he is coming soon!

Table of Contents

Foreword

If it weren't for my friendship with Kelly Carroll, I don't think I would have even considered a 40 day fasting and prayer journey. She led the way with her vibrant, joyful, encouraging spirit, and we became prayer partners during this special time. In this book, she shares her personal journey through the 40 days of fasting and prayer in an honest, inspiring way that will encourage you, but be warned, you may be moved to action yourself. You won't regret it! Kelly's passion for the Lord and hunger for more of His Spirit and anointing is evident to all those around her. She has a tangible energy from the Holy Spirit that lifts the atmosphere of a room with the love of the Lord. I have seen Kelly serve faithfully in many capacities in the local church and community being a blessing to so many with her heart of compassion. She is a faithful friend, a dedicated mother, and grandmother, a gifted artist, and an accomplished business owner. Kelly is a woman who walks with God and is intimately acquainted with the Holy Spirit. She is not afraid to share what God has put on her heart. She is not afraid to dream big for herself, but most importantly, she will dream big for others. In reading this book, I know that you will be blessed by her testimony of God's faithfulness.

I was with Kelly Carroll when I first heard about the 40 day fast and I have to admit, my first reaction wasn't to jump for excitement. I actually had an adverse physical reaction to the table where the "Fasting" books by Jentezen Franklin were sitting. I didn't want to go near the table. I didn't want anything to do with it. The more excited she got about fasting, the more annoyed I became at the whole idea. I wasn't used to having a reaction like that so I paused to assess the situation and the Lord spoke to me. He told me that I was having a physical reaction in my flesh because learning to cultivate a lifestyle of prayer, infused with fasting, would release supernatural freedom and power into my life like I had never seen before. I realized when God spoke to me that I was afraid that I would fail. I was afraid that I would not be able to complete the fast and frankly, I had no idea if it was even possible. The Lord was about to show us that it was possible! Kelly had the faith for what seemed impossible and she looked me in the eye and told me that I could do this … that we were going to do this together. I was about to embark on a great adventure that would cause freedom to be loosed within me in the most powerful way!

Let's face it … fasting and prayer is something that you have to *decide* to do in your spirit and set your mind to with determined focus. You have to *believe* that the Word of God is true and that the power He released when His people fasted and prayed in the Bible will also be released into our lives today! I didn't know this until I recognized that the Lord speaks about practicing the discipline of fasting and prayer in the Word. I could no longer ignore fasting as an important aspect of the Christian walk. Let Kelly Carroll's powerful testimony encourage you to get rid of limitations, inspire you to go deeper with God, and believe that you can do ALL things through Him!

—Gentry Dinsmore
Director of Career Services
Lecturer at Pioneer Pacific College

Introduction

But the time will come when the bridegroom will
be taken from them; in those days they will fast.
Luke 5:35 (NIV)

There was a time in my life when God had me in a place
I called "the darkroom." It is not a place of darkness where
evil awaits you or where you should be afraid. Sometimes
it seems so or feels that way. But maybe it is a place where
you need to be still and wait on God. My darkroom was
the place that God took me to and left me there for a time
(a very long time, consisting of years!) of development. It
was not necessarily a happy room or pleasant place for me
to be, but it was required by God so that he could do the
work in me needed to develop my negatives and what I
call my gifts and character. It is similar to going through
your peaks and valleys of life. But this time, it just felt like a
darkroom where he had me rest, be still, and know that he
was there. It took me years to know that he was there with
me. It is when God takes us to our lowest and most desper-

ate moments in our life that his voice can be heard, and it is there that he will speak into our life. God said to me that we are not captives—that Jesus came to set the captives *free*! I love how the Old Testament intertwines with the New Testament in introducing our Savior, Jesus Christ.

> The Spirit of the Lord God is on Me, because the Lord has anointed Me to bring good news to the poor. He has sent me to heal the brokenhearted, to proclaim liberty to the captives, and freedom to the prisoners; to proclaim the year of the Lord's favor, and the day of our God's vengeance; to comfort all who mourn, to provide for those who mourn in Zion; to give them a crown of beauty instead of ashes, festive oil instead of mourning, and splendid clothes instead of despair. And they will be called righteous trees, planted by the Lord, to glorify Him.
>
> They will rebuild the ancient ruins; they will restore the former devastations; they will renew the ruined cities, the devastations of many generations.
>
> Isaiah 61:1–4 (HCSB)

God knows what he is doing, and we should never question him in our moments of despair. However, I did a lot of questioning. Have you ever noticed that when you question God, he becomes very quiet and very still? That is when you feel like screaming, "Why?" But if we become still and quiet with him, we hear his voice.

The darkroom is a very important place that God had me sit. My life in God's hand was much like the photographer who toils and works hard to take the perfect picture in the perfect light, with the right speed of film, during the most beautiful lighting times of the day or night. He then takes his film to the darkroom. In order for a picture to be developed, you must first start with a negative. It is there that he shuts all the doors so no light can get in, except his light, then he gently and carefully removes the film from the camera, unrolls it, and prepares it for developing in solution on photo paper, with only the low red lighting to see it develop (I envisioned this as the blood of Jesus covering my life). He then takes the photo paper out and hangs it to dry (this was my growing and maturing time in our Lord). Once the photo dries, it is stable, then it is processed and ready to handle the light. That was when God took all my negatives that I had went through in my life and turned them into positives.

God works on us in similar ways. When he has us in the darkroom, we should never rush him to give us all we want immediately, and most of the time, what we want is not always the best that God has waiting for us. We might not be ready for what we are asking of him, and we would totally get overexposed like film when it is pulled too soon into light, leaving the picture unclear, blurred, or even ruined and overexposed. If we rush God into his plan for us or get ahead of God, we will not see the full measure of his glory. It is for his glory that we strive to do his will, after all. Sometimes we even push our own plans ahead of God, squashing out the true blessing that is waiting for us if only we had waited on him.

Are you waiting on God and feeling like he is far away or not hearing your prayers? We all have been there and felt desperate and unheard. Dear beloved, know in your heart right now that God hears every word, every cry, and sees every tear you give to him. Meditate on these scriptures for strength, and speak the Word of God out loud, and watch God move on the words you speak aloud!

> Wait on the Lord;
>> Be of good courage,
>> And He shall strengthen your heart;
>> Wait, I say, on the Lord!
>>> Psalm 27:14 (NKJV)

> I wait for the Lord, my soul waits,
>> And in His word I do hope.
>>> Psalm 130:5 (NKJV)

> And we know that all things work together for good to them that love God, to them who are the called according to his purpose.
>> Romans 8:28 (KJV)

> God Will Be Gracious
> Therefore the Lord will wait, that He may be gracious to you;
> And therefore He will be exalted, that He may have mercy on you.
>> For the Lord is a God of justice;
>> Blessed are all those who wait for Him.
>>> Isaiah 30:18 (NKJV)

Before I began writing this book, God put into my heart a strong desire to know him more intimately and visions for my future with a hunger for his presence. I had a hunger so strong that my soul ached to know him deeply. I read my Bible, prayed, was a cheerful giver, sought after godly friendships, and the list could go on. I was desperate to know the what, where, when, and why purpose of my life.

God called me back to himself in 2006 after turning my back on him for over twenty-six years of selfish rebellion, drinking, drugs, and living for my own gain. All through the years, I always heard that ever-so-still voice of God speaking to my heart. One night, in my lonely despair, I finally broke down and fell to my face before the Lord. It takes desperate measures sometimes for God to get our attention, but when he does, he knows that his timing is the best plan for our life. He knows everything about us, every thought, and every sin behind closed doors, and he still loves us.

Over these past few years, I have experienced the love of Christ sweeping through my life, teaching me who I am in Christ and how his plan for my life is for the glory of God. He has taken my mess and promised to me that it will be my message for his glory and his honor, proving that miracles and salvation are for anyone and everyone. The Bible says that whoever calls on the name of the Lord shall be saved! "Believe in the Lord Jesus, and you will be saved, you and your household!" (Acts 16:31, NASB)

This is a story of a journey that God took me through in order to get me to a place of submission and true worship. His grace and his power are ever present in my life now, and because of his awesome love for me, all glory and honor will be his.

I believe with all my heart that I am destined and called to share the gospel with a true love for Jesus Christ. A love I have never felt before so strong in my entire life. So powerful and so complete is his love for us that no matter what we go through, I know that he is with us. He has called me his daughter and has given me visions that have become a reality of truth in my heart.

Straight from the mouth of Jesus, he says …

> And He said to them, Go into all the world and preach the gospel to all creation.
> He who has believed and has been baptized shall be saved; but he who has disbelieved shall be condemned.
>
> Mark 16:15–16 (NASB)

God is so ever present in all we do, if we open our soul, our hearts, and our true worship to him. I believe we do, in fact, live in the last days. All you have to do is look around you and see that the world is in a tailspin of despair, brokenness, sadness, and with no hope for things to get better. With Jesus, all things are possible! His blessings are for whomever he finds available to do his will. He is truly looking for individuals who seek him from the heart. Just as it says in 1 Timothy 1:5, the goal of this command is love, which comes from a pure heart and a good conscience and a sincere faith (NIV).

I love this scripture below because if you know anything about computer e-mails and sending phone text messages and such, you know that when words are all typed in capital letters, it is a signal of yelling! In the NASB, this passage is in all caps, as if God is speaking as loud as he can to those who will hear his voice!

> And it shall be in the last days,' God says,
> "That I will pour forth of My Spirit on all mankind;
> And your sons and your daughters shall prophesy,
> And your young men shall see visions,
> And your old men shall dream dreams;
> Even on My bondslaves, both men and women,
> I will in those days pour forth of My Spirit
> And they shall prophesy.
> "And I will grant wonders in the sky above
> And signs on the earth below,
> Blood, and fire, and vapor of smoke.
> "The sun will be turned into darkness
> And the moon into blood,
> Before the great and glorious day of the Lord shall come.
> "And it shall be that everyone who calls on the name of the Lord will be saved."
>
> Acts 2:17–21 (NASB)

I pray for the Holy Spirit to be present within the pages of this book and that his anointing will sweep the pages as you read this for God's glory only. I never really considered myself to be a preacher or teacher. However, God has called me out to become separate from the world to share the good news of the gospel and the saving grace that is found by having faith in Jesus Christ, our Messiah.

God is an awesome God! If he can pull me out of the clutches of Satan, save me, and redeem me from all my sins (which were numerous and horrible), then he can do anything. He chose me … wow, what a thought. I did not choose him, but he chose me to be a fully devoted disciple of Jesus Christ! A daughter of the King Most High!

If you don't have Jesus Christ in your life and you choose to or refuse to accept the truths in God's Word, you are never going to live in Heavens eternity. God wants all of us to come to him. But we must accept Jesus Christ as our Lord and Savior and believe he came to die for us so we would have life eternal.

There is a real place called heaven and a very real place called hell. Jesus actually talks a lot about the things of hell and the things of heaven. He does not want anyone to perish but all to come to repentance.

When you repent, the Lord will remove the veil and show you his truths. Which would you choose? All you have to do, with a willing heart, is ask Jesus to come into your life and take over your heart, and he will!

If you want to experience a new life in Christ and let him transform your life, then pray this simple prayer below.

> Jesus, I want you to know that I am sorry for all I have done in my past. Please forgive me. Please come into my life and change my heart and show me your way, your truths, and your love. I promise to follow you the rest of my life. Jesus, thank you for giving your life for me on the cross. Show me now the way you want me go and how I need to become the best I can be for you. In Jesus's name. Amen!

I believe that if you just prayed that with a sincere heart, you have just been born again. That means you are a new creature in Christ Jesus. The Bible says if you ask the Lord to come in … he will!

> Behold, I stand at the door and knock; if anyone hears My voice and opens the door, I will come in to him and will dine with him, and he with Me.
> Revelation 3:20 (NASB)

Your next step would be water baptism and to get involved in a local church. Any church you choose should teach directly from the Word of God, the Bible, and be alive with God's spirit.

Praise the Lord! Here are a few scriptures for you to think on … and don't forget to get a Bible and read it every day to renew your mind in his Word.

He loves you!

> Jesus said to him, "I am the way, and the truth, and the life; no one comes to the Father but through Me."
> John 14:6 (NASB)

> Therefore if anyone is in Christ, he is a new creature; the old things passed away;
> behold, new things have come.
> 2 Corinthians 5:17 (NASB)

The Day Before...

It's Mother's day! My kids took me to Timberline Lodge for a five-star brunch afternoon. Prior to lunch, I spent the morning snowboarding with my son in spring conditions on the mountain that looked no different than a winter day on Mt. Hood. It was snowing, actually pelting us hard, and twenty-six degrees. It was a bit chilly and damp and no doubt a spring-like snow with winter conditions. Mt. Hood had over 203 inches of snow still and just might get more before the summer is here.

We snowboarded for a couple of hours, talking a bit about the Lord. I always talk with my son about salvation. God has shown me how open he is to him. I can't imagine spending eternity without my kids with me there. That is the one thing that saddens me most is to think of them in eternal hell if they do not fully devote their lives to Christ. It was at that moment that I felt the call of God to fast for my kids. I love my children so much. It gives me great joy spending time with them as grown adults. We grew up together and successfully made if through all the hard times. I did so many things wrong while they were grow-ing up that I don't understand how they have turned out so completely wonderful. They are the biggest and most joyful people in my life. God loves them, and because I am a daughter of the Most High, I must take action in prayer now—like right now!

We never know when our time is up on this planet or when we will meet Jesus face-to-face. We do not know or understand how many days we are given and that they are numbered. Life can take us out at any given moment. My fast is foremost for the salvation of my kids. For them to spend eternity in heaven with Jesus rejoicing with them and giving praise to our Lord forever together.

Our brunch was a beautiful time spent with my son (his wife could not make it), my daughter, her fiancé, and my grandson-to-be.

We ate till our hearts were content. I indulged in fresh seafood, prime rib, fresh veggies, salads, breads, fruits cov-ered in chocolate from the chocolate fountain, and then desserts. It was too much food to be eating before my fast, but it all was so wonderful.

Two years ago, God delivered me from a life of drink-ing almost every day when I would come home from work. It was a way to cover the loneliness and despair I lived with most of my life. Years of drinking and years of living life in the fast lane was a habit hard to break. It is actually a yoke of bondage that Satan loves to drag people around in. I gave it to God, but somehow Satan was able to sneak it back into my life slowly, gradually, making it appear that it would not be a problem anymore. The problem with it was that it would squash out the presence of God in my life every time I had even one glass of wine.

Wine makes the mind dull, relaxed, and creates the wanting for more. It makes you sleep, slumber, and not think of the things of God. It creates thinking for the world. It makes you lazy.

We live in the world, but we need to be separate from the world. I believe that Jesus is coming back for us in this generation and in our very lifetime. His Word tells us to be clear minded, alert, and waiting on his arrival. He wants us to keep our lamps burning bright for his arrival.

I know he loves me. I know he is with me, and I pray every day to find a way to walk only for him. Well, he called me out to do just that.

He said to me, "I will make you a disciple. *You will go through changes of unpleasant reproof and training, and you will fast to break every yoke of bondage on you and your family!*"

When I heard those words, it was powerful, loud, and clear. He has promised to send me out to you who are reading this book right now, to prodigals who have returned home to his kingdom, and to others who need to hear the good news of the gospel; and yes, it is *good news!* He can take anyone's life and redeem it, change it, and fill it with the goodness that only comes from our Savior, Jesus Christ. He has turned *my mess into a message for the world*. Praise him, and all glory to him who died for me!

Amen.

After thoughts

We all have our reasons for fasting—whether it is for biblical reasons, answered prayer, or for improved health. My driving force was propelled forward when God's Holy Spirit said to me, "I have given you the power to ask for all things, if you believe." Those words stuck in my head for hours one day as I heard God's voice tell me this over and over. He also said that my power would come from prayer and fasting together. I have never fasted for anything more serious than what I was about to take before the Lord.

My family is covered by yokes and bondage for as far as three or four generations back (the words God gave me in a vision). These yokes have kept our family in bondage of a prison that consisted of abuse, abandonment, prescription drugs, street drugs, alcohol, divorce, disease, illness, selfishness, carnal living, non-believing lifestyles, and family dysfunction.

First and foremost, my prayers and fasting have been offered up for my immediate family. As you read earlier, my family has been subjected to all of the above, and it trickles down to each generation and keeps on going, like a ripple on a lake, or stays connected for years, like a linked chain.

I am fed up with the bondage and the enemy who controls all the life-altering destinies. I decided it was time for a serious prayer war in fasting. God knows my seriousness of breaking free the loved ones in my life. Breaking free so that we all will have salvation, freedom, and learn to rebuild and restore what God's original plan was for our family!

These are my personal journals of my forty-day journey for freedom. I wait in expectancy for the miracles to unfold and God to be over us and to break the chains Satan has over this family.

If you have a desperate need for change and for God's power to take over and rein in your life and your children's children, then consider the power of praying, giving, and fasting together.

God's grace and his power were my only source of strength to do this. I am nothing without him! Praise our Lord, Jesus Christ!

These are the personal notes, journals, and thoughts that fell into my heart as each day passed. As you read, you will find the true and lasting spiritual love that comes from the Father.

The power of prayer is awesome, and as I recorded all these prayers and thoughts, I cried when I reread them for myself as I put them here on these pages.

> Father, I pray in Jesus's name that you fill these pages with your Holy Spirit and let the prayers within this context reach out to the lives reading them. May they uplift and fill hearts with hope and understanding of how real you are and how much you long for us to need you in a desperate way. Thank you and praise you for all your goodness and faithfulness. In Jesus's name. Amen!

Day One

I went to bed last night, knowing very well how my first day might leave me feeling. I was shaky and lightheaded most of the day. I had Queen Headache show up because of lack of food, and I felt extra hungry from the huge meal the day before. Satan was on my back: "Eat ... eat ... eat ... it will make you feel better!" I refused, and I drank water—and lots of it. I sipped on chicken broth and some watered-down apple juice. Between all this, I was challenged to have to work. I work hard grooming pets and driving all over the city in my mobile van. Grooming is very physical and demanding. I was weak and tired when I got home that night. I lay in bed and wrote in my fasting journal. I prayed that God would give me mercy and grace to get through to the next day ... and he did.

> The acts of the sinful nature are obvious: sexual immorality, impurity and debauchery; idolatry and witchcraft; hatred, discord, jealousy, fits of rage, selfish ambition, dissensions, factions and envy; drunkenness, orgies, and the like. I warn you, as

I did before, that those who live like this will not inherit the kingdom of God.

Galatians 5:19–21 (NIV)

Fasting has brought me into a deeper and more intimate and powerful relationship with the Lord, even though I am only into the first day. Maybe because of the commitment and heartfelt need to seek him in such a way as this. As this day comes to a close, I do know that when I eliminate food from my diet for many days that my spirit will wake up and becomes uncluttered by the things in this world and my mind is amazingly sensitive to the things of God.

"I am seeking you, Lord—your grace, your blessing, and your will. Show me what to do. Save my kids. Take away all my unhealthy habits and crush them. All I want is you, Lord."

> Therefore be careful how you walk, not as unwise men but as wise, making the most of your time, because the days are evil. So then do not be foolish, but understand what the will of the Lord is. And do not get drunk with wine, for that is dissipation, but be filled with the Spirit.
>
> Ephesians 5:15–18 (NASB)

After Thoughts

As my journey began, I started to really hear his voice speaking out. God spoke to me and said, "I am going to do a new thing in you." He called me out for fasting and prayer. My original plan was to fast for twenty-one days.

My very dear friend Gentry was not excited to jump into this journey with me, but I needed a fasting and prayer warrior to be accountable to. She said no at first but called me on day three of my fast and said to me, "I'm in." So the journey began that day, not knowing the impact and blessing that was coming in alignment with God the Father, Jesus, and the Holy Spirit.

I really like how The Message Bible describes this chapter of Isaiah 58 concerning fasting and the worship of God. It can't get any clearer than this:

> Shout! A full-throated shout! Hold nothing back, a trumpet-blast shout! Tell my people what's wrong with their lives, face my family Jacob with their sins! They're busy, busy at worship, and love studying all about me. To all appearances they're a nation of right-living people. Law-abiding, God-honoring. They ask me, "What's the right thing to do?" and love having me on their side. But they also complain, "Why do we fast and you don't look our way? Why do we humble ourselves and you don't even notice?"
>
> Well, here's why:
>
> The bottom line on your *fast days* is profit. You drive your employees much too hard. You fast, but at the same time you bicker and fight. You fast, but you swing a mean fist. The kind of fasting you do won't get your prayers off the ground. Do you think this is the kind of fast day I'm after: a day to show off humility? To put on a pious long face and parade around solemnly in black? Do you call *that* fasting, a fast day that I, GOD, would like?

This is the kind of fast day I'm after: to break the chains of injustice, get rid of exploitation in the workplace, free the oppressed, cancel debts.

What I'm interested in seeing you do is: sharing your food with the hungry, inviting the homeless poor into your homes, putting clothes on the shivering ill-clad, being available to your own families.

Do this and the lights will turn on, and your lives will turn around at once. Your righteousness will pave your way. The God of glory will secure your passage. Then when you pray, God will answer. You'll call out for help and I'll say, "Here I am."

If you get rid of unfair practices, quit blaming victims, quit gossiping about other people's sins, if you are generous with the hungry and start giving yourselves to the down-and-out, your lives will begin to glow in the darkness, your shadowed lives will be bathed in sunlight. I will always show you where to go. I'll give you a full life in the emptiest of places, firm muscles, strong bones. You'll be like a well-watered garden, a gurgling spring that never runs dry. You'll use the old rubble of past lives to build anew, rebuild the foundations from out of your past. You'll be known as those who can fix anything, restore old ruins, rebuild and renovate, make the community livable again.

If you watch your step on the Sabbath and don't use my holy day for personal advantage, if you treat the Sabbath as a day of joy, God's holy day as a celebration, if you honor it by refusing "business as usual," making money, running here and there...

Then you'll be free to enjoy GOD! Oh, I'll make you ride the high and soar above it all. I'll make you feast on the inheritance of your ancestor Jacob."

Yes! God says so!

Isaiah 58:1–14 (The Message)

Spring was approaching, and my hunger for more of God was like the same hunger I am experiencing while fasting without food. Except that God's hunger is more deeply engrained in my soul so much that it seems there is nothing that will satisfy this insatiable desire to have more of his presence in my life. The Lord has been gracious to me, with mercy on top of mercy as I cried out for more. He called me to a fast—a fast that would fill a different hunger and create a fleshly hunger I have never in my life endured. When the stomach growls, the flesh dies, and your spirit is fed. Satan screams and fights with anger, because he knows that victory is about to triumph in the life of someone who endures God's will.

Fasting breaks years of chains, yokes, strongholds, and burdens. It is the breakthrough of prayers that sometimes go unanswered. Fasting gets God's attention, and he hears. It does not get you brownie points with our Lord because you fast. You must fast for a purpose and a sacrificial reason of your total and complete worship. One thing to always remember is that God wants your obedience to Him more than He wants sacrifice. Fasting is obedience to Him as He calls you to this task. Fasting is a stepping stone and a tool God gave us that will open the heavens. It speeds up our prayers to heaven for help to break the barriers that hold us captive. It gives the angels huge assignments to minister for the good of the saints.

Before you consider a fast of any kind, you should consider your health, consult with your doctor, and always make a sound choice of the kind of fast you are about to journey on. I don't recommend a fast for anyone if it is not called of you by our Lord.

Please check with your medical professional for advice on any choices you decide.

There are many fasts you could do. A complete fast with no food or water (consult your doctor) or a fast of only water. Some fast with clear liquids, like clear soups and juice and water. There is the Daniel fast in the Bible, where Daniel fasted on vegetables, water, and no wine. Do your homework, and follow God's plan—not yours.

This is the beginning of my journey—the fast God has placed in my heart—and as I write my journey out and share my prayers, weaknesses, and challenges, you will learn also that our strength and grace to endure comes only from him!

I am making Jesus my Lord, not Lord stomach, and putting aside the ever Miss Queen Headache when she comes.

I am expecting and waiting for miracles, signs, and wonders to take place; to see yokes of bondage removed from the history of my family, because with Jesus, all things are new; and to walk into victory with the salvation of my children's children.

> Now to Him who is able to do far more abundantly beyond all that we ask

or think, according to the power that works within us, to Him be the glory

in the church and in Christ Jesus to all generations forever and ever. Amen.

Ephesians 3:20–21 (NASB)

Day Two

I woke up feeling empty inside physically, overjoyed that I made it twenty-four hours with no food. I prayed on the side of my bed before my feet hit the floor that Jesus would be with me today, keep me from temptation, and give me grace to endure another day.

I walked in the kitchen and stood there, wanting to fix my morning yummies. It is such an engrained habit to do the day's routine of waking, eating, and going to work. We just don't realize how habits affect our lives and how hard they are to break. I somehow am understanding the yokes that God breaks in our lives when we have the strength that he gives to us to break our own yokes of habits for his glory.

So I stood there in the kitchen, thinking of food only—ahhh ... hot oatmeal with blueberries, a cup of juice, and toast.

"*No!*" my spirit yelled at me. I settled for a cup of coffee. I have been allowing myself one cup of bistro coffee from my Starbucks machine in the morning with a little milk and no sugar. That is all I get to indulge in. My body will be fed only water, clear soup broth, and watered-down juice in order to keep up some strength. I am allowing this because of the demands of my work. It by no means has suppressed my *hunger*! *God*, be with me, give me grace, hope, and peace as I go to work today. Let my hunger be a reminder of my reasons for fasting.

Let today be a reminder of the patience I will need to endure to get through nineteen more days of hunger, which will lead to a deepening spiritual awareness with our Lord, Jesus Christ, as my prayers breakthrough to heaven.

I love the way The Message Bible describes the patience and endurance it takes to walk with Christ and what it means to endure for him. This is total and complete worship, sacrifice, and commitment.

May God give me mercy as I try not to look at the days ahead but learn that it is day by day, glory to glory, and minute by minute that I walk in his love.

> By entering through faith into what God has always wanted to do for us, set us right with him, make us fit for him, we have it all together with God because of our Master Jesus. And that's not all: We throw open our doors to God and discover at the same moment that he has already thrown open his door to us. We find ourselves standing where we always hoped we might stand, out in the wide open spaces of God's grace and glory, standing tall and shouting our praise.
>
> There's more to come: We continue to shout our praise even when we're hemmed in with troubles, because we know how troubles can develop

passionate patience in us, and how that patience in turn forges the tempered steel of virtue, keeping us alert for whatever God will do next. In alert expectancy such as this, we're never left feeling short-changed. Quite the contrary, we can't round up enough containers to hold everything God generously pours into our lives through the Holy Spirit!

Christ arrives right on time to make this happen. He didn't, and doesn't, wait for us to get ready. He presented himself for this sacrificial death when we were far too weak and rebellious to do anything to get ourselves ready. And even if we hadn't been so weak, we wouldn't have known what to do anyway. We can understand someone dying for a person worth dying for, and we can understand how someone good and noble could inspire us to selfless sacrifice. But God put his love on the line for us by offering his Son in sacrificial death while we were of no use whatever to him.

Now that we are set right with God by means of this sacrificial death, the consummate blood sacrifice, there is no longer a question of being at odds with God in any way. If, when we were at our worst, we were put on friendly terms with God by the sacrificial death of his Son, now that we're at our best, just think of how our lives will expand and deepen by means of his resurrection life! Now that we have actually received this amazing friendship with God, we are no longer content to simply say it in plodding prose. We sing and shout our praises to God through Jesus, the Messiah!

Romans 5:1–11 (The Message)

As my day comes to an end, I am focusing once again on the things that matter most in this fast. I'm fasting to break the yokes of bondage in my life, my kids' lives, and my family for financial freedom and God's will for my life. I want to know what I am here for, what God's will is and what the reason is for all my past troubles I went through and how will it turn out for the glory of Jesus Christ and God the Father! I struggle mostly with the desire to bury my worries and pains in that tasty glass of wine I so dearly made my friend for so many years. I ask the Lord to break that yoke and set me free. My stomach growls and pains me—and to think, this is only day two. Nineteen to go!

I am learning how to sacrifice and not worship my stomach! But God has had me hanging in the darkroom, developing me for great things. I don't dare open the door until he is done with me. I am like film in a camera: we take the pictures (that is our vision), God then removes the film (that is our prayers being heard), and he places our film, pictures, in his solutions under the red light (that is the blood of Jesus), and he slowly develops us.

> Therefore, I urge you, brothers, in view of God's mercy, to offer your bodies as living sacrifices, holy and pleasing to God, this is your spiritual worship. Do not conform any longer to the pattern of this world, but be transformed by the renewing of your mind. Then you will be able to test and approve what God's will is, his good, pleasing and perfect will.
>
> Romans 12:1–2 (NIV)

This journey seems hard and long, but I follow the one who did it before me because he left and went to the Father to prepare a great place for me. He did this so that I would be blessed with his power to do what he did and even greater things, if I believe.

We must go through the valleys to stand tall on God's mountain—or through our darkrooms of life in order to come into the light. I sometimes wonder why I turned my back on God for over twenty-six years and ponder what my life would look like today if I continued to serve him back then. Then all of a *sudden,* God said to me, "*Never, never look back.* You might turn to a pillar of salt, like Lot's wife!" Wow, what a great way for the Lord to remind us to press on to the future, not looking back because he has thrown our mistakes as far away as the east is from the west. Praise him who cleanses me.

God's words came to my mind in Matthew 19:30 (NKJV): "But many who are first will be last, and the last first."

I am the youngest of five kids. God spoke to me and is preparing me to be the first. I pray for discernment on that for my life. Maybe I am the first in my family in over four generations who is serious about my fasting and prayer to break bondages on my family. I will be the first to change a whole future generation to come. Let the captives free, Lord.

Set me free as well, Lord, from the long years of loneliness that have been a yoke of oppression over all my family and me.

Let your conduct be without covetousness; be content with such things as you have. For He Himself has said, *I will never leave you nor forsake you.* So we may boldly say:

> *The Lord is my helper;*
> *I will not fear.*
> *What can man do to me?*

Hebrews 13:5–6 (NKJV)

As we fast and pray, we need to desperately hang on to faith in what we are asking for and praying for. Our faith is a wonderful worship up to our Father. As you pray, believe in your worship to the Father that he hears every word you submit to him. What better promise is there than this:

> Most assuredly, I say to you, he who believes in Me, the works that I do he will do also; and greater *works* than these he will do, because I go to My Father. And whatever you ask in My name, that I will do, that the Father may be glorified in the Son.

John 14:12–14 (NKJV)

As I press on for my hunger for Jesus instead of my hunger for food (even though my body tells me, "Eat!"), I will only look to heaven for my spiritual food and guidance to the everlasting food and water that will never leave me hungry or thirsty. Blessed are those who hunger and thirst for righteousness, for they shall be filled (Matthew 5:6, NKJV).

When we fast, it is not a time of real joyful experience because you are actually in a lot of pain (hunger pains are just that—painful). In James, it says to grieve, mourn, and wail. Change your laughter to mourning and your joy to gloom! I don't know of any other way to do those things or how they really make sense; however, fasting is just that.

So I think this is a description that fits our total bodily worship to God. It gets his attention when you submit your whole body, mind, and spirit. I will press for the prize of my prayers to reach heaven.

> Therefore submit to God. Resist the devil and he will flee from you. Draw near to God and He will draw near to you. Cleanse *your* hands, *you* sinners; and purify *your* hearts, *you* double-minded. Lament and morn and weep! Let your laughter be turned to mourning and *your* joy to gloom. Humble yourselves in the sight of the Lord, and He will lift you up.
>
> James 4:7–10

After thoughts

> Come now, and let us reason together,
>> Says the Lord,
>> Though your sins are as scarlet,
>> They will be as white as snow;
>> Though they are red like crimson,
>> They will be like wool.
>> If you consent and obey,
>> You will eat the best of the land;
>> But if you refuse and rebel,
>> You will be devoured by the sword.
>> Truly, the mouth of the Lord has spoken.
>
> Isaiah 1:18–20 (NASB)

As I pondered upon this scripture, I realized the power in it and just how much the blood of Jesus over me has made me white as snow. He had a plan and a purpose for my life, and I did not obey. I did not experience the best God had for me for many years. It took total brokenness and awareness of his hand on me to send me to the depths of my own despair and unworthiness. I began to realize how insignificant I was in the world and how powerfully beautiful and useful I am in his kingdom. Without him, I am nothing; with him, I am everything he wants for me and has in store for me.

When Satan knows that God has a powerful plan for your life, he will work overtime to try to snuff us out, lie to us, keep us far from God, and blind us from our true identity and purposes that are waiting for us to fulfill for the glory and power of God's kingdom! We use our own reasoning and self-doubts to sabotage God's real power that awaits us. If we would just consent to God, he is faithful in breaking us free from our own ways, our idols, and our selfish agendas, and *he* will give us the ability and the grace to walk out our obedience, but we must listen first in order to hear him. He is powerful and faithful—think on that always. He wants to fill us to the full while Satan is trying to devour us. But greater is he that is in you than the one who tries so very hard to distract or derail us from our purposes God has for us. We are children of God, and when we turn our lives over to him completely, great things happen. "You, dear children, are from God and have overcome them, because the one who is in you is *greater* that the one who is in the world" (1 John 4:4, NIV).

So now what? Choose to eat the best of the land, what God has for you. Do not refuse God, and then you will know that it is impossible to be devoured by the enemy! All things are possible with God! Truly if you listen, the Lord will speak.

Day Three

It was a very hard night. I did not sleep well at all, waking up every couple of hours. It was almost like spiritual warfare going on all around me. My senses were so aware of every noise in the house, outside the house, and I could even hear my own blood pumping through my body.

I was extremely hungry throughout most my day. Sometimes hunger pains were intense. Smells were so vivid as I drove through town, smelling the different restaurants. My mouth was dry, and my tongue felt fat and pasty. Mints were needed, for sure!

Hunger changes the course of all your thinking. Your whole day is focused on how you will get through the next hour. It causes your spirit to reach out to the Lord every minute of every second. Prayer is constant, vivid, and it actually feels wonderful at times as you feel your spirit connecting with God.

This is the longest I have ever gone in my entire life without eating. I am weak and tired but, at the same time, energized by the Holy Spirit. It takes all I have left in me at the end of the day to go home after work and do anything around the house. But I did mow the lawn after work today. It was a physical challenge being hungry. Energy is okay, but I feel like I am detaching from my daily focus. It is definitely a spiritual journey.

I am preparing for my trip to the beach with my daughter. I pray for strength to get through the weekend because I know I will be surrounded by food.

Jesus is the source of my strength, and I need to remind myself that I can do all things through him who gives me strength. Philippians 4:13 (NKJV) says I can do all things through Christ, who strengthens me.

As I approach into the evening, I smile with wonder and amazement of the grace God has given me to get through the first three days. They have not been pleasant. Jesus knows the sacrifice of hunger and pain. He bore it all for us. He fasted forty days, and after he fasted, he preformed miracles, then came his death on the cross for us.

Jesus is my Lord and Savior. I will pray every day for grace to walk in his ways and complete the task ahead as my love goes out to the Father. I know this will be my time of development and knowledge of his purpose for my life.

Praise him!

After thoughts

God redeemed me from the pit of hell, and I am going to lay it all out because it is my truth and redemption. I have learned that those who confess their sins one to another are truly redeemed. It's all a part of declaring our testimony of how God saved us. As I started my journey, fasting for answers and to experience breakthroughs and miracles, I somehow found myself writing, journaling, and praying for hours and very extended times.

God showed me that praying is the very thing he wants us to do all the time, every day, and as a complete and wonderful form of worship. We should praise him in our every waking moment. I decided to give him my forty days completely without distraction or retraction. I also turned off that horrible television and found that the time spent alone with God was life changing.

This is truly the beginning of a new walk with the Lord who loves me and has called me out of a life of destructive decisions, lifestyle, and disobedience.

God showed mercy and grace to me as He changed me and made my life new. He is all powerful and wonderful. His salvation brings healing. He made His presence known to me. His sensitivity toward me filled me with value and worthiness. Glory to God in the highest!

I will again reaffirm the voice of God through Isaiah 1:19–20 of my first encounter with the Lord when I heard his voice tell me "if you consent and obey" that I would eat the best of the land. Wow, what a word from God. His word is not only a promise, but it is true, and it is for you too. It is power and it is victory for every person when it is applied and lived out in your life.

> If you consent and obey, You will eat the best of the land; But if you refuse and rebel, You will be

devoured by the sword. Truly, the mouth of the Lord has spoken.

Isaiah 1:19–20 (NASB)

It is hard for me to begin my story. But yet it is cleansing for the soul to unveil the darkness that had a stronghold on my family and me, probably before I was born.

I believe this scripture in Jeremiah with all my heart, and it resonates deeply in my soul, knowing that God is faithful and his promises are true.

> For I know the plans that I have for you, declares the Lord, plans for welfare and not for calamity to give you a future and a hope. Then you will call upon Me and come and pray to Me, and I will listen to you. You will seek Me and find Me when you search for Me with all your heart. I will be found by you, declares the Lord, and I will restore your fortunes and will gather you from all the nations and from all the places where I have driven you, declares the Lord, and I will bring you back to the place from where I sent you into exile.
>
> Jeremiah 29:11–14 (NASB)

The Lord has totally brought me back to the place where he sent me to remind me of where he is taking me today. His grace is an awesome free gift to all who will call out to him. He wants to shower those who seek him with his blessings and reveal to us his will.

God had his plan for me long ago, and the ways of the world choked out his plan and his assignment for me in my life due to my own selfish desires, lust for worldly things, and not focusing on the things of God. It is so true that he wants the best for us because he knows us—he *really* knows us—more than we know ourselves. He knows our thoughts before we think of them. He knows the mistakes we will make ten years from now but offers his amazing grace over us if we so choose to walk in the ways of our King.

> For You formed my inward parts;
> You wove me in my mother's womb.
> I will give thanks to You, for I am fearfully and wonderfully made; Wonderful are Your works,
> And my soul knows it very well.
> My frame was not hidden from You,
> When I was made in secret,
> And skillfully wrought in the depths of the earth;
> Your eyes have seen my unformed substance;
> And in Your book were all written
> The days that were ordained for me,
> When as yet there was not one of them.
>
> Psalm 139:13–16 (NASB)

My days were already planned by God. However, I did not follow the plan God wanted me to walk in, but he knew well in advance what road I would travel, and he knew exactly what it would take for me to fall to my knees and repent. I don't blame my circumstances or my parents, but I know that because of strongholds that are over our families, it can affect us in every area in life and give way for the enemy to attack! When we listen and submit to God's calling and resist the devil, he eventually will flee.

Be of sober spirit, be on the alert. Your adversary, the devil, prowls around like a roaring lion, seeking someone to devour.

1 Peter 5:8 (NASB)

The thief comes only to steal and kill and destroy; I came that they may have life, and have it abundantly.

John 10:10 (NASB)

Before I begin this story, I will tell you that God has placed in my heart a gift of forgiveness. I love my family, my mother (who is now with Jesus), and I especially love my father today like I have never loved him before. That in itself is a gift from God. They are my only parents I will ever have, and I honor them for the life they gave me and that I am here to give my testimony. My testimony is not to hurt those who read it but to bring healing because God's salvation heals. I once heard someone say that "unforgiveness is like drinking poison and expecting the other person to die." Forgiveness is not for the other person; it is for you to release bitterness from your heart and give it to God to deal with (and he will). When you do, then you gain life. Life comes abundantly, and a life that holds a healthy heart for all of eternity has much to give others. We will touch more on the act of forgiveness in a later chapter.

When I was a very young baby, less than two years old, my mother and father separated, and my mother chose to walk out on five kids, leaving us with our father to raise us. Being so young, I do not remember her leaving, but I do remember her periodic visits back to see us and the feelings of her leaving and knowing she would not return for months. It was so sporadic and far between visits that I didn't even remember what she looked like by the time I had reached the first grade of school. Abandonment stays with us, even into adult life. But I will rejoice in Psalm 27:10 (NIV): "Though my father and mother forsake me, the Lord will receive me."

I grew up with three older sisters and an eldest brother, with me being the youngest. And being the youngest meant I always got all the hand-me-down clothes and hand-me-down everything. By the time I did get the clothes handed off to me by my sisters, they were worn out. I did not care if they were old, worn-out clothes because they were new to me.

My sisters practically raised me; in fact, they actually did raise me. My father worked for the railroad and was constantly gone on long trips for days at a time in order to support five kids. My brother was the oldest, and I was the youngest of my other three sisters. My father was stern, strict, and downright mean at times. I cannot count the many times I was beat and I watched him beat my sisters with his belt, his fist, or his open hand. We were all afraid of him. He was like the wrath of God, and when we did not do what was right in his eyes, all hell broke loose. We were his housekeepers and his cooks. He imparted upon us physical and mental abuse at different times throughout our childhood, not knowing what the long-term affects were going to be in our future lives.

I recall one time when Dad was home from work and my sister and I were sitting side by side on a small couch off the dining room, which was joining to the living room. It was there my dad had his recliner chair and always sat in it to read the paper. As he sat down, he instructed us to go get busy on the dishes in the kitchen. As a simple little argument started between my sister and I, all about who was going to wash the dishes and who was going to dry them, my dad interrupted us and said he didn't want to hear another word. My sister's elbow found itself in my side as she nudged me over and over to not argue. And of course, I had to get the last word in, and that struck a nerve in my dad. He jumped out of the chair with his hand drawn back, ready to strike me, and I took off running through the dining room, around the corner, and into the kitchen. As he ran in pursuit of me, he fell as he tried to run around the corner on a freshly hand-waxed floor. In his anger and humiliated attempts to hit me, and the fact that I ran, his rage was sent to a level I wished I would have never seen. As I ran myself into a corner in the kitchen, he brutally picked me up and threw me against the backdoor that led to the backyard, kicked me several times, hand fisted me in the face, and then beat me with his belt that left welts too numerous to count from my legs all the way up my back. The next morning, I woke with a black eye and bruises on every limb of my body. The worst memory for me was the embarrassment the next morning as he made me get dressed for church and went like nothing had happened. After that day, I was beaten down emotionally, as well as physically, to the point where I did not feel worthy of love. I even had a low self-esteem throughout school with friends and held an inferior image of myself. I was afraid to assert myself in any public situation. And if I was challenged or forced to stand before my classmates to read or do anything, I would tremble in fear from the inside out. Those days have long passed, but the crushed spirit within followed me throughout my life from that one-time event. It was nothing more than abuse and torture. My heart goes out to the children of this world that are beaten, hurt, and abused. Just one time will make a child different and damaged for life. Jesus didn't intend for our world to have hurting children but to love them and protect them. My prayer goes out to all of you who have had similar experiences, and I want you to know that people hurt us, but Jesus heals us. And sometimes the ones that hurt us are the ones right under our own roof.

Because I was a little girl who grew up without a mother's touch in my life, I developed a hard exterior of protection. I did not know what it felt like to have a mommy tell me I was a beautiful little girl or have that gentle touch of her hand brushing my hair. I was raised with a stern hand, as if I were a boy (and I am sure boys need a mom's gentle touch as well). There was one day that I was given boys' underwear by my father because he said that they were brand new and someone gave them to him for free, and he expected me to wear them. I cried and cried in humiliation of how I was going to explain this when I went to school and had to undress for gym class among my friends. As a girl, it really affected my self-esteem, and my deserve level to ever feel feminine had been destroyed. I felt unworthy of love and that my father did not care enough about how badly I felt. That is a hurt that lasted into adulthood. If I felt shame and unloved from my earthly father, then how is it that I was able to connect to my spiritual Father in heaven and believe he cared about me and wanted to give me good things? I did not have those thoughts or feelings. I remember praying to God as a little girl a lot, and I knew he heard me because he did answer prayers in small things. But I never knew how much he loved me and how much he was always there with me through all the troubles and loneliness.

My father did take us on a couple of vacations that I remember to California to visit aunts, uncles, and cousins. I remember our trip to Disneyland and several camping trips where I was taught to fish. He was the only source of family all of us had, and those are the only good memories I held close in my heart as a child. I cherished those times, and it was my foundation of love during those *moments* that kept my heart within the family circle. I loved my daddy as a little girl, no matter what had happened or what was to come. We were taught to never question how he treated us or talk about the things he did to us kids behind closed doors. We continued to sweep these things under the rug all the way into our adult lives.

I remember growing up, feeling all alone. I was very much alone most of the time, left for hours in an empty house. I recall a time when I was hungry, and because I was so young, I had to stand on a chair to reach to the stove to cook myself some oatmeal. My sister that was closest to me in age was four years older than myself. Because all my sisters were four to ten years older, it seemed I was left to grow up on my own accord. There was a family that helped take care of me for a period of time before my school days started that extended into the first and second grade. I hated being there, but I had no options.

I remember having a friend who would come to visit me when I needed someone near the most. Her name was Teresa. I spent a lot of time with her. She had to have been an angel sent by God to watch over me, minister to me, and protect me, because my sisters never saw her, and they teased me that I was always talking to an invisible friend that I made up in my head. They thought it was because I was alone, but yes, I was alone and very lonely, so I believe with all my heart that God took care of that. "Are not all angels ministering spirits sent to serve those who will inherit salvation?" (Hebrews 1:14, NIV)

Teresa was always very quiet and would let me do most of the talking, which I still do in real life—one of my weak areas I pray God will give me grace to listen more! She always seemed to be the same size as I was, no matter what my age was. She was always dressed in beautiful dresses that were brilliantly colored with flowing material that would drape perfectly over her and move gently with her body. There was always some sort of lace on her sleeves, at the bottom of her dress, and just under the hem as well. Her hair was long, wavy, and light in color. She wore a hat with a ribbon around it, and it never fell off her head.

When I got older, around six years old, I was playing around in the bathroom in the sink, talking to Teresa, and one of my sisters needed to use the bathroom and was getting angry with me to come out. She finally came roaring in and sat on the toilet, and I started to cry. She asked me what the problem was, and I told her she crushed Teresa. I only got laughter from my sister, and she tried to hug me, but I was mad. After that day, I never had a visit from Teresa. I think the Lord used that day to take that time with my angel and put her to work somewhere else. But I believe it was an important time in my life that God provided for me. I wonder to this day if my sisters ever really believed me that I had that special visit from God's angel to protect me in such a time like we had growing up.

When I reached eight years old, my father had met a woman and then married her when I was nine years old. At first, it was kind of fun having a new woman around to do things for me. I had never really known what that was like. She made me clothes on the sewing machine that I *hated*! She also made me clothes for my Barbie dolls (that I still own today). She gave me my first (and only) birthday party I ever had in my years growing up. Things seemed like they might be okay. Little did we know that she detested all of us kids. She did not like us around after my father married her. She even told my sister that she hated us. She almost divorced my dad months later because she could not handle raising someone else's kids. Late one night, my sister (the one closest to me by four years) and I were listening through the crack in our bedroom door to my dad and stepmom arguing over us. She told him she did not love us, no matter how hard she tried. She said she could not stay because of us. My dad was crying and begging her to stay, so she did. However, it did not take long for her to get rid of us one by one over the next few years.

Before all this came about with my stepmother, my oldest sister was already gone because she had gotten married when I was eight years old. My next sister was the first to go; my stepmom did not like her, and I remember my dad finding anything he could to beat her and accuse her of doing wrong all the time. She ended up going to live with my oldest sister to finish high school. I never really understood why she left.

It was just my one older sister and me left at that point, and that too didn't last long. One day, my dad was in a rage because my sister left the horse lead out and didn't put it in its proper place. He came storming in the house and threw it on the table and said, "She is going to get a beatin !" When my sister came home, Dad was working on something in the yard, and I ran and told her that she was going to get beat! She took one look at me and said, "*No more* ... not anymore," and went in her bedroom and grabbed a few things and ran out the door. She never moved back home again after that day and went to live with a new family where she felt safe and loved. I still would see her from time to time. But I missed her so badly. So it was just me left at home, and I felt that same lonely feeling all over again that I had when I was younger.

As time went by, I was not getting along with my stepmother at all. By then I was thirteen, and she was a thorn in my side. We would argue and fight when my dad was gone to work or not home, and when he got home, she would tell him I was bad and unmanageable. Of course, he would beat me, ground me to house arrest, and make me feel horrible. I somehow got the courage to find out where my real mother was and begged my dad to find her phone number so I could contact her. She was in Rochester, New York, and I was in Oregon. I finally got her number from my dad. And so after contacting her, I told her my story and how I was being treated over the years, and she agreed to let me come to New York and live with her. I am sure my dad was in a state of relief getting rid of us all because of my stepmother's abhorrence toward us.

I flew out to New York and did not even know this woman called my mother. I did not know what she looked like; no one had a recent picture of her, and the worst part was that I had no idea what I was getting myself into.

It was a new adventure being only thirteen years old. I was in eighth grade and failing school so leaving felt good at the time.

After I got there and met my mom and my stepdad, I tried my best to settle in and convince myself that this was home. They spoiled me when I first got there with a whole new wardrobe, because the clothes I was sent with were not fit for any young girl to have to present herself in. I started school there, and things were going quite well with new friends. After all the years of feeling inferior, I suddenly had a new heartfelt change of acceptance from all these new people at school. I was the new kid from Oregon, and everyone wanted to know me. My grades in school were not good in Oregon at all, and it took hard work and a few months to see the change for the good. I felt a sense of accomplishment for the first time in my life. After completing the rest of the year there in middle school, I made the transition to high school at Brighton

High. It was a huge school and a new, scary beginning that I embraced and looked forward to, even though it terrified me. I was doing fine for the first time ever that I could remember. Then things changed for me within that first year at high school because my stepdad tried to fondle me in an inappropriate manner that really caused a lot of confusion and distress in my new life. All the fear of physical abuse and torment came back to me in one instant. It was like a flashback but without the bruises.

I was so scared that I packed up my stuff and went to a friend's house and refused to come home. My mom did not believe me when I told her what he tried to do to me. She was angry with me and said it embarrassed her. She finally convinced me to come home after three days; when I did, she had all my bags packed and took me to the airport and put me on a plane, right in the middle of my first year in high school. I was so confounded with grief because I had made friends there at my new school, my grades were good. I had my first boyfriend, a good-looking Jewish boy who was a junior at our high school. Not only was I disheartened about being sent back to Oregon, I was also very sad and depressed to leave all the things from school, my friends, and my mom again. I felt abandoned by my mother in a more severe emotional trauma than everything prior to knowing her.

It was abandonment in the worst degree. I felt unworthy, unloved, and even hated. I felt that nothing good would ever come of my life. Everything was meaningless and hopeless. Not only had I been abandoned as a baby, but again by my father when he remarried, and then again a third time by my mother when I was at a crucial age as a teenager. I was, in essence, a walking hormone looking for direction.

The trip home was very depressing and disappointing. I cried most of the way home.

The airline attendant kept bringing me sodas and snacks, trying to console me and raise my spirits, but it did not work. When the jet approached the time we would be landing back at Portland Airport, I focused on the fact that I would be going back home to my dad's house with him and his wife, whom I did not want to even be with or look at. So I was thankful that, at the very least, I had a bed to sleep in.

I got off the jet plane and met my dad. Then we walked to get my luggage. He never talked much to me the whole time until we got in the car. We were driving on the freeway, and he started to tell me that I couldn't come home because if I did, his wife would divorce him.

I sat there in shock, thinking, *Where am I going to go live then?*

So I asked him how he could do this to me. "I am your daughter. Where am I going to live?"

He told me that there was a home for kids like me.

I said, "Kids like me? What do you mean?"

It was a place for kids to live when they had no other place to go, called the Attention Home—not a de-tension home—because I did not do anything wrong that deserved punishment.

I was placed there and became a ward of the state of Oregon. I felt unloved, unworthy, loathed, and pushed aside—like he was throwing me away. To this day, I don't understand how any parent can dump kids off like people dumping pets off at an animal shelter. That's how I felt.

After three months in the attention home, I was placed in my first foster home. It was temporary—and then another and then another. The last foster home was a place where I lived with several other girls. It was a bad situation, and the man of the house drank a lot and was molesting some of the girls. My life was spiraling into a pattern of rebellion. I had no direction, no sense of family, and no love or encouragement. I grew up with no mother to comfort me and teach me the things a young girl needs to know. I never was taught how to manage my life problems at school, how to handle my money, and what it meant to have any kind of life goals. No one cared, so it seemed. I would come home from school and just sit in a chair and stare for hours sometimes and have anxiety in my chest. I felt like my chest was in a vice because I worried about where I would end up. I hated being in the care of strangers who had no love or concern for my feelings or fears.

One night, one of the other girls and I got a great idea to run away and get the heck out of there. I did not care where we ended up at the time. I was sick of everything, everyone, and was not worried about my future any more since no one else was worried about me either. We left in the night and ended up on a highway, hitchhiking. We were picked up by a couple of older guys in their forties maybe. I don't know, but they could have been older.

We traveled with them for quite some time, all throughout Idaho and Montana. We finally had to stop and get motel rooms because it was so late. They were nice enough to give my friend and I separate rooms, but they were adjoining rooms. I ended up getting raped by the driver that night as he entered my room through the access door. It changed my whole life. I remember the look in his eyes, and it was so cold. I was a virgin, and he knew it. I will never forget the dirty, shameful feeling it left inside me that night. I never told my friend I was with because of that shame.

It took about three months for my sister to find me and convince me to come back home, and when I did, I moved in with her because she was closest to me, and I knew she loved me. I became rebellious and defiant—not with her, but with life. I did what I wanted when I wanted to and did not care whose toes I stepped on to get what I needed in life. Independence became my first name, and self-government was what ruled my every decision. I was drinking alcohol, smoking pot, and taking drugs of any sort to experiment with anything that would make me high. By the time I had reached fifteen, I convinced my counselor (who tried her hardest to make me believe in something) to go to court and ask the state to emancipate me as an adult. I learned quickly that emancipation meant that if I were to get into any trouble at all, I would be treated as an eighteen-year-old adult. So the state of Oregon emancipated me, and life began for me at a very early age.

At this point, I was a damaged adult in a kid's body. I was forced to grow up, hiding behind a pretty face, without looking beat-up emotionally. I was so psychologically expired at an early age that it was hopeless for me to ever depend on anyone in life, except on my own efforts for a better life.

A few months had passed, and I met a guy that took interest in me, and like a magnet, I stuck to him. It was the first time I can remember that anyone would want me and want to keep me. I clung on to him for dear life, and within three months, we were living together, and I had quit going to school. My sister had a fit because I was still living with her at the time when I met him. My father even took me aside and said I needed to get rid of him because he was too old for me and was not a good influence in my life. I laughed at all of them and said he was the only one who really loved me. He was nine years older than me, and back then, when I was young, no one did anything about it since I was emancipated, nor could they. In today's society, that would have been considered statutory rape.

Our life together consisted of partying, smoking pot, drugs at times, and lots of drinking. We both worked, and he was starting a business of his own in the auto body business. He was driven by the pleasures of life and material things of this world. He actually became obsessed with making money.

After two years together, I became pregnant at seventeen, and we were married before the baby came. I had my first son at eighteen.

Life changed for me when I became pregnant. I stopped all the partying and took care of the baby and myself. I was really into the healthy diet and looking for better ways to raise this new baby that was about to change my whole life.

However, my husband was still doing life the way he always did from the time I met him.

I started going to church and gave my heart to Jesus at the age of nineteen. Soon after that, I was baptized, and I worked hard at learning what it meant to be a new Christian. I was never mentored or taught the understanding of baptism and what it meant to be baptized, but I believe that God's Holy Spirit took my life in his hands, knowing where I was really heading, and it was right then, I believe, that God decided to never let me go.

At twenty-one, I became pregnant with my daughter. After her birth, I had stopped going to church and was right back in the ways of the world. I had no support from my husband to continue serving and living a life within the church. I had no roots developed for Christ and did not stick it out for very long because of all the past things in life I had already experienced from my family life. All my life, everything ended up being unfulfilling and never lasting long enough to know what it was like to have roots in family, church, and especially God. How could God love me that much anyway (that is what I used to think)? I did not want to believe that it was an eternal way of life, because there was not one thing in my past that ever lasted when it came to love.

After years and years of miscommunication with my husband, our relationship broke down, I had become very unhappy and despondent. If we had a fight or I didn't do the things he expected me to, he would not talk to me for two or three days. At the time, I was teaching aerobics and had a dance studio where I held my classes. It was the only thing that held my emotions together. After returning home one weekend from a fitness conference in

Oklahoma, I shared my excitement with him that I was chosen and offered to be on the cover of *Shape Magazine*. They wanted to feature me as a mother, wife and fitness instructor for that month's issue. He told me in his discouraging voice, "No, I wouldn't count on becoming somebody." It was at that moment that I knew I would leave him. A year later, I left for a couple of weeks and flew back east to New York and stayed with my sister for a time to get away. I made a decision that very week that changed my life, and it seemed as though I was on a one-way trip to hell. I met a man and ended up staying with him for one night. That one night changed my whole life from the inside out. I felt so horrible, and my mind was attacking me with guilt and unworthiness. I came home from that trip and delivered the news of divorce to my husband. I never dreamed in a million years that I had it in me to betray him, even though I was so tired of the marriage problems and the lifestyle. I felt as though he never listened to me or ever really loved me. My infidelity destroyed me from the inside out. I have never told anyone about this through all the years as they passed by, and my own kids never knew. God was dealing with me back then, but I ignored His voice. I was young and spirited inside but yet so broken and had no life skills that anyone ever taught me growing up. I could not comprehend what it meant to stick it out and make it work, because all my life, everyone just left me to my own accord and pushed me away. So the logical thing was to divorce and start over, even though my husband expressed his desire to work it out. I still walked away because it was all I knew and all I ever had happen in my past. I was terrified to tell him what I had done because the rejection from him would hurt me more than leaving him. I can't look back on what might have been, but I do know God would have taken it in His hands if I listened to His voice.

I am classic in the prodigal daughter story, as my life unfolded into a disastrous and careless lifestyle.

I turned to the world of fun and parties once again. Even though I loved my kids, continued to raise them, and tried my best to care for them, I still let all the world's fun overcome me, and Satan had his playground all laid out before me. And as the years went on, he had a field day trying to destroy me.

I married three more times between 1988 and 1999. I only got a glimpse of love, and that was with the second marriage. But it was love without Jesus. I married out of loneliness and despair but, at the same time, was deeply and genuinely in love with my new husband. The one person I thought who would never hurt me did so when I found him with another woman. As much as it hurt, I believed it was God's punishment to me for what I did in my first marriage and what I was hiding. This time I even stayed for almost another year, trying to work it out. The pain of the betrayal was too much for me to handle, and without the help of God, it was just not possible for me. "…with God all things are possible" (Matthew 19:26).

After this divorce, I went almost nine years single. I moved to San Diego and lived the great life (I thought), with parties, the beach, the sun, and all the fun the world offered. But it is only for a season, until it all crashed down around me. As my world began to collapse, I sold everything I owned and went back to Oregon for a short time.

Life back in Oregon was not working out financially after trying hard for a year, so I left and moved to Florida with my daughter. (Let's run away from our problems, right? It worked when I was a kid.)

In Florida, I seemed to settle and get financially more stable with my daughter (my son was already eighteen and had moved out), and we were far away from past problems. I found work there and then soon opened my own sunglass shop on the beach. It was fun, exciting, and no one was there to remind me of my past. It was there that I met my next husband.

My third marriage was filled with the world's passion and infatuation for riches and money and status that Florida is famous for. I did not marry for love at the time and for the person or husband he was or could be but for what he had to offer. This man had money, and he spent ridiculous amounts of it on me. That made me feel special and wanted, temporarily. He was very controlling, outright verbally manipulating, so much that it scared me. Our lifestyle was a big part of a lot of drinking and the party life in the midst of the rich and famous. I did learn to love him deeply, even among all the troubles and dysfunction that engulfed my life from drinking too much. After a few months into the marriage, he accused me of infidelity, lies, called me names, and said I needed help. Instead of a loving approach, it was very passive aggressive. I remember a few days before Christmas we were in bed and his cell phone rang, and I picked it up from the table on my side. As I looked at the Caller ID, it read a woman's name. I handed him the phone with no questions because I didn't dare question *his* behaviors. He had a conversation with a woman in bed with me whom he was apparently seeing that I did not know about. When he hung up I asked him who it was and he said to me, "You don't want to know." I felt hopeless, and my life was in despair with the feeling of no way out or help for the feelings that inundated my brokenness and downcast, discouraged spirit. It eventually led me to try and take my life with prescription drugs that were prescribed to me from my doctor. That very night in my despair, I lay in the bathtub and drank wine with a handful of pills. As I slowly began to fall into a deep sleep, I knew I would not come out of it alive and would be meeting someone on the other side of life that scared me. Then I heard a voice and saw a man sitting on the edge of the tub. It was Jesus. He said to me at that very moment, "I am not done with you yet," and then I felt his presence so strong inside my spirit, as he gave me a hopeful feeling. I remember asking him to forgive me for doing this to myself. It felt like it was too late, but Jesus knew my heart was broken and shattered beyond my own control.

God always has a different plan when we are hopeless and broken inside. His plan is not what we expect. We can't even begin to conceive what God is about to do for our life when we reach the bottomless pit. He has the ability to reach us and pick us up so we can finally see him and His glory that he wants to bestow upon us in those moments.

I remember waking up in a room with a strange man sitting in a chair. He just looked at me and asked me, "Are you going to try this again?" I told him no, and he believed me after I told him my story, so he released me from the hospital. After my recovery from having charcoal forced in my stomach to absorb the drugs and a few days rest, I moved out of the mansion on the water, packed a small bag, and was on the road to divorce once again. I felt failure yet relief, because after dating a year and a half, the marriage only lasted six months. During the months of waiting for the divorce to be final, my soon-to-be ex-husband had locked my daughter and I out of the home from getting any of our personal things. My daughter and I lived with two sets of clothes. We had two of everything and had to wash our other set of clothes every other day. He would not let us get my furniture or anything during this time. We slept on the floors of our new house with blankets and pillows borrowed from a friend. We had bought two plates, two of every kind of utensil, and a couple of pots and pans to cook from. My neighbor let me borrow a thirteen-inch television, so we had some kind of evening entertainment together. It was a very difficult time, but I somehow gathered up from deep inside my soul enormous strength and a new level of patience. The divorce would have been quick, but this man was suing me for bigotry. He was convinced that I was not divorced from my last husband. My attorney told me that if we did not find my divorce papers, I would be doing jail time and even asked me if this man planned out how to try to ruin my life. I never really knew why he was so mean and could not understand why he was doing all this to me. It all was very confusing. My attorney finally closed the divorce and countersued him for the distress he caused me. It gave me enough money to buy a better car and get on my feet with a new job. After the final signing of papers he told me he found a box of my things and I could come and pick it up. When I got to his house I took the box and thanked him. He looked at me with sad eyes and said, "I still love you." I looked at him with a blank stare and said to him, "You are the one who needs help." Three weeks after our divorce was final, he married the woman he had the phone conversation with while laying in bed with me that night before Christmas. I was exhausted and worn out emotionally.

Oh, and again, here we go around the mountain one more time, I remarried yet another man only after a year and a half. (You think this is a pattern of desperate loneliness? Oh yeah!) I was beginning to go to church, and he did too, so in my own fleshly need, I took him as my husband, knowing it was not of God. I was still living a pattern and lifestyle of drinking to cope. Things were wrong from the beginning, and I knew in my heart that there was an evil about this relationship; and yes, it was abusive once again. I always seemed to pick verbal and damaging relationships that struck me down in my spirit, and my self-esteem had no room to cope with anything in my future, let alone deal with my past problems that were still within me. I was no rose petal to live with either at this point, as I began to retaliate these moments and episodes. It was not in me to be angry and fight, but I had no other options left, and my mind and soul were just plain worn out from my own bad choices. I often wondered why I chose to be with men who were abusive, mean, and unloving. I became very cold inside my heart and blocked out the pain to protect myself from a total breakdown again.

At this point in life, all the failures from my past surely did not make one more divorce any different than the one before. Life felt hopeless. I felt literally hopeless. I would think to myself that all men were selfish, mean, and out for their own gain. What I did not see was that I was outside of God's plan for my life. I was living in sin and did not want to admit it or submit to it. Without Jesus, my choices were all wrong. He had a plan and a future for me, and I chose not to follow that path, and it was for that very reason everything fell apart all along the way in my life. It was the reason I did not have the protection and the God-given wisdom over me, helping me to make those important decisions. God just stands back and lets us fall sometimes until we get the senses knocked out of us so that we can see how much we *need* him.

I finally moved back home to Oregon. As I settled there and opened a business and began my life, things looked normal for me and felt normal, and I had a sense of peace and financial relief. I still drank a lot at times to relieve loneliness as the world sees fit, and drinking socially with friends was my way of not having to be alone with myself. On the outside, I looked like I had it all together, and on the inside, I was scared, lonely, and burned out.

I bought property in 2001 and had dreams and hopes of living a normal life. I began the process of trying to get together the right plans to build my dream home in 2004, and then I met a man one night that said he would help me build my home.

We started dating, and like all the past relationships, I began with being sexually active inside that relationship (not God's plan). At the time, it was the only way I felt I could feel love. Then we began the process of excavation and building my home. During the course of that year, our relationship deteriorated off and on. Our relationship was wrong from the beginning because he was only separated and not divorced, and it led to a lot of problems along the way. With the sexual immorality in a relationship like this, God's protection and blessings are far removed.

When the house was done, I did not allow him to live with me (God was beginning to deal with me, and the Holy Spirit was calling), and we ended the relationship. As time went by, I found myself missing him, and we would talk long hours on the phone. As time passed and our physical separation became reality, he ended up with another girl-friend, and it left me feeling so abandoned, hurt, lonely, confused, desperate, and so much more I can't even explain.

I was hopeless, living in a brand-new home, with a life most people only dream they could have. People looked at me as a girl who made it all happen for herself, a hard worker, a girl who had her act all together, blessed—you name it. But it was not the real me. If someone were to ask, "Would the real Kelly please stand up?" It would be a broken-spirited, lonely, scared, pathetic-looking, shameful woman who was disgusted with her life. That is the type of person I felt like inside, standing before the world and before God.

I knew I loved Jesus, but I loved the world more. I had one foot in the church and one foot in the world. It was not working. I was not living the life God had planned for me. I believe that the Lord kept me in his will all those years of disobedience and had his hand on me, refusing to let me fall completely from his grace and his plan for my life. Because he came to me in my despair one night and said in an audible voice that almost scared me enough that I thought someone was in the house (at least is seemed audible to me!), he said "Do you want rest?" And I cried out, "*Yes!*" It was at that moment I broke down and cried and asked him to come into my life to take over and never leave me and not to forsake me as all of life had done.

All my life, I pictured God standing above me with his arms crossed while pointing his finger at me and tapping his toe, saying, "I am very mad at you for all you have done!" God is a loving God, and what he really was trying to say to me is, "My heart has been broken for you and for all that you have had to go through as a child, but you have been destroying yourself, but I have a solution for you. I have sent my Son to pay for all of your mistakes and sins. He wants to heal you, and he has taken all your sin and shame away, and now I do not see it. But you must follow my ways and not your own because I love you." When this revelation was given to me by God, I suddenly realized the *power* and *glory* that was involved in my salvation and that I am the daughter of the *King*! He plans to use my messed up life for the good and for the glory of *him* and *his* kingdom.

The Lord Jesus changed me that very night from the inside out and cleansed my heart from so much trouble in my past. He delivered me from a very deep-seeded loneliness. I have learned that I am washed white as snow and that I am seated at the right hand of Christ. I am a new creation, and if I am to ever love another man again in this life, Jesus has given me the strength to practice purity, and I am now willing to follow all the precepts of the Bible with courage and strength, as well as a willing heart, to be obedient to him until he says it is his timing to have that one true life partner come into my life of his choosing! I will no longer choose to do my own will, but *his* will be done in my life.

Satan comes to kill, steal, and destroy us, and he almost succeeded. But not without a fight from our glorious Lord fighting for me. He loves us that much! People hurt us, but Jesus came to save us and heal us so that our joy may be full! I am letting Jesus be my romance and my first love—now and forevermore. He will never leave me or forsake me! He will teach me purity, and he has totally forgiven me.

The book of Hebrews teaches us exactly what he wants.

> Marriage should be honored by all, and the marriage bed kept pure, for God will judge the adulterer and all the sexually immoral. Keep your lives free from the love of money and be content with what you have, because God has said, Never will I leave you; never will I forsake you.
>
> Hebrews 13:4–5 (NIV)

I will continually thank our living God in heaven for sending us Jesus Christ, who has forgiven even "my" sins, as horrible as they were.

Nothing is impossible in Jesus Christ. His love and his power rule the earth and can change your whole life, only if you open the door for him to come in.

I encourage you to ask him and invite him into your life, heart, mind, and soul today.

Day Four

I woke up, and before my feet hit the floor, I prayed. "I slept!" Wow, it felt good to sleep and wake up feeling this good.

I pray for grace each day. I am off to work to groom dogs. Only thing I take is my four bottles of watered-down juice.

On the trip to my first appointment, I was stopped at a construction spot in the road. I was the first in line, so I had visible view of the gal holding the stop sign. She was looking right at me, smiled, and then reached into her cooler next to her and pulled out a *huge* floppy piece of pizza and was chomping big bites. As I watched her, I was thinking to myself, *Hmm ... she must be working for the devil.* It was just funny to me because everywhere I went, I smelled food, I saw food, and thought of food. That is when you just start praying for more ... more ... more *grace.*

I get to go to the beach for two days. Praise him.

My prayer for tonight, Father, is protection for Heidi, me, Tara, and all the girls during this festive party at the beach. Protect us, and give me your anointing to take with me out to the places I will go.

In Jesus's name. Amen.

G'night.

> In You, O Lord, I put my trust; Let me never be ashamed;
>> Deliver me in your righteousness.
>> Bow down Your ear to me, Deliver me speedily;
>> Be my rock of refuge, A fortress of defense to save me.
>> For you are my rock and my fortress; Therefore, for Your name's sake,
>> Lead me and guide me.
>> Pull me out of the net which they have secretly laid for me,
>> For You are my strength.
>> Into Your hand I commit my spirit;
>> You have redeemed me, O Lord God of truth.
>>> Psalm 31:1–5 (NKJV)

> Behold, I am with you and will keep you wherever you go, and will bring you back to this land; for I will not leave you until I have done what I have promised you.
>> Genesis 28:15 (NASB)

After thoughts

I want to share with you that over the past several years, I have had to cope with the lies from Satan about my worthiness and right standing with God about feeling worthy of loving another man in a marriage relationship.

I have had people, pastors, and friends judge my life history, as if it will always be tainted and dirty.

God has taken my life and made me whole. I know who I am in Christ Jesus, and by repenting and truly loving him in truth and spirit, there is forgiveness.

He did die for us and shed his blood so that we would be made whole, clean, and white as snow to start over. If he did it for Moses, who murdered, and for King David, who committed adultery and murdered tens of thousands of people, then he will forgive you and me.

> Therefore if anyone is in Christ, he is a new creature; the old things passed away; behold, new things have come.
>
> 2 Corinthians 5:17 (NASB)

> Therefore we have been buried with Him through baptism into death, so that as Christ was raised from the dead through the glory of the Father, so we too might walk in newness of life.
>
> Romans 6:4 (NASB)

Who am I in Christ Jesus? As Christians, we need to always remember who we are in Christ Jesus. It is powerful to speak scriptures over your life every day. Satan is the father of lies, and he wants more than anything to take away your self-esteem, your confidence for Christ, and your identity. He wants to kill all that is working in you from the Lord, and he wants to destroy you on a daily basis. Don't ever think that you are exempt or immune to his attacks. He is the enemy! Satan especially hates women. We have to stop and remember that the fall of man started with Eve. Satan was thrown out of heaven from his rebellion and haughty attitude that he was going to be greater than God. He also was the most beautiful angel in all of heaven, and I believe he has a vengeance upon women because of the tender beauty God bestowed on them. He tempted Eve because she was the most beautiful creation that God had made. He is struck by the heel of Christ, who also was born of a woman. So until women can confidently rise above to know how beautiful and powerful in Christ we are, we will struggle to find victory and healing. There is healing and victory in the Word of God. Please know there is power as well in speaking the Word of God out loud over your life. His words and his promises are a double-edged sword, and Satan can't stand to hear them spoken. He will flee.

There is no cost but a lot of rewards in praying the Scriptures. Let's continue to pray for one another. Here is a prayer you can pray over yourself and over your loved ones who are in need of the touch of Jesus Christ.

> Father, I ask you to bless my friends, relatives, and everyone reading this right now. Show them a new revelation of your love and power. Holy Spirit, I ask you to minister to their spirit at this very moment. Where there is pain, give them your peace and mercy. Where there is self-doubt, release a renewed confidence through your grace. In Jesus's precious name. Amen.

Day Five

I woke up to find your presence with me, Lord. My task for this day is on my mind, but I spent my time in prayer with you. The Holy Spirit was with me. I am empty physically, and hunger pain is constant but not painful today.

God will take my prayers up and answer them for committing to this fast. It kills the flesh—hunger makes you more aware of God's presence. Hunger and the empty feeling in your stomach and your soul draw you near to God. It opens your mind like a vivid sensor, full color and in stereo. You can hear him ...

I packed for the beach, praying for grace to be with me and strength to wrap around me as I spent time with eight other young women at the beach who do not walk in the ways of your ways, Lord.

It was a good day. The girls are crazy, fun, and so beautiful, and I pray for mercy on all of them as I endure my fast, praying that I am a light in a dark place for them to see.

Evening fell on us with such beauty that only God can create. Clear skies wander over the roaring ocean as God tossed the sea back and forth. A setting sun in clear view of God's light shining on me. He is good.

As night fell and I sat on the beautiful deck overlooking the ocean with my daughter-in-law and her friend, we were speaking together about the things of God. They are sensitive toward God's presence, but I pray for a miraculous awakening in all my family—one that is from on high and full of power and grace from the Holy Spirit. Praise be to Jesus.

Day six begins soon.

> How lovely on the mountains are the feet of him who brings good news, Who announces peace and brings good news of happiness, who announces salvation, and says to Zion, "Your God reigns!"
>
> Isaiah 52:7 (NASB)

Day Six

The roar of the sea put me to sleep as the ocean air gently breezed in through my window last night. It is easier to sleep now. Matter of fact, my sleep has never been sweeter than it has been so far. I am beginning to feel a deeper, more real presence of God. I am settling into a comfortable satisfaction of my fast for him. Hunger still reminds me that the flesh tries so hard to rule over me. When we kill, the flesh the spirit comes alive, and it awakens to new things.

God is able to reach out to you and speak to your heart. The Holy Spirit never leaves you when you are deep in a fast and combine it with a lot of praying! The unimportant things of the world fade away, and worries and concerns are not in your thoughts because the peace of God is all over you! You know and understand that God is in control.

My faith and trust are at new heights. I feel freedom and life and blessings springing forth in faith. I know now that I can do all things through Christ, who gives me his strength.

God is light.

This is the message which we have heard from Him and declare to you, that God is light and in Him is no darkness at all. If we say that we have fellowship with Him, and walk in darkness, we lie and do not practice the truth. But if we walk in the light as He is in the light, we have fellowship with one another and the blood of Jesus Christ His son cleanses us from all sin. If we say that we have no sin, we deceive ourselves, and the truth is not in us. If we confess our sins, He is faithful and just to forgive us our sins and to cleanse us from all unrighteousness. If we say that we have not sinned, we make Him a liar, and His word is not in us.

1 John 1:5–10 (NKJV)

My desire is to walk with Jesus and walk in love and in his light for all time. I need you, Lord, every day!

I walked the beach in the warm sun, listening to praise music. God spoke to me many times. I feel unspeakable joy! I would not turn back at this point in my fast, because his presence is clear and vivid today, and the joy I have is like nothing I have experienced. When I prayed or worshiped before this fast, the Holy Spirit would come, and I would feel a lot of emotions and love for God, with a heartache of tears and reverence. But today, the Father showed me that when you offer up your body as a living sacrifice, there are no barriers between your spirit and the Holy Spirit…he is then able to get inside you completely and ever so sweetly minister to your soul in ways that bring real and lasting joy with a glimpse of the things to come!

Tonight is the last night at the beach. I had soup at dinner with all the girls. I was diligent and asked my waitress to remove all the chunks of veggies out and just give me the liquid. She was gracious. Tomorrow I can't wait to go to church and be in God's house. I never get enough of his presence in my life—I long for it every minute. Father, please take care of my every need as I lean on you for the next two weeks. *God is good*!

On the way back to the beach house after leaving the restaurant, we had a divine intervention or angel encounter of the Lord's protection! I was in the backseat with my daughter, and my daughter-in-law was driving, and her friend was in the front seat, all talking, and we were attempting to turn left across Highway 101 in a turning lane. Suddenly, a car came around the corner in our lane, heading straight at us head-on, going very fast, so we swerved to miss the head-on car; and as we did, a car from behind missed by fractions from rear ending us at the same time! As the car from the front missed us and the rear car flashed suddenly from the rear by my window, all the girls turned to me when we stopped and said, "We have angels with us! Thank you, Mom, for fasting and praying this weekend!"

At that very moment, I knew God was with us, and I realized that I prayed for protection for our travels two days prior to this event. God is good. I have been a bright light for all the girls, because they believed it was my prayers and angels with us that protected all of us. It was a miracle.

I did not want to really share with them that weekend that I was fasting and praying, because that was a personal thing with me and the Lord, but being with them all weekend, I had to let them know why I was not eating and feasting with them. They respected it, and it was a witness of faith in our Lord to them—a brighter light than all the world could shine and a louder message of hope for salvation than any words could speak to them. I believe in salvation for every one of those girls I spent time with that weekend. Thank you, Lord Jesus.

Day Seven

The sound of the ocean crashing was in the background of my dreaming. I did not want to wake up. I knew this was my last morning to wake up to such beautiful surf, but I had to get up. My body is tired today. But eagerly, I rose up to go home, go to church, and seek God and try to somehow get life back on track. Vacation is good.

I spent much time in prayer. I am hungrier today than I was on my third day. The headache has returned, but I did not have my usual cup of coffee (my one cup a day, which I shouldn't but do).

I sang praise music all the way home. I am what you might call "in the zone" today. I had a hard time focusing at my belong class at church. I am learning about my new place God has planted me. I plan to root down there like a tree. It was a day that was difficult to stay in prayer or write. God is telling me to work diligent and hard and keep writing. I pray for his spirit to be in these words you read to give hope, understanding, and a new grace to all who are touched by the Lord through fasting and praying.

I took some amazing photos of the ocean while I was there. The sunsets remind me of God's light, his goodness, and his power.

Oh, my stomach pains me today. My craving to eat was strong. I slept for a couple of hours this afternoon, then went to the store, and it exhausted me.

Father, I pray for the strength that only you can supply to fill me up tomorrow for work. I love you, Lord. I wait on you and your voice. Your presence is already here—praise God! I am going into day eight!

After thoughts

As I stated earlier on, I once heard that unforgiveness is like drinking poison and expecting the other person to die.

It took me years of hurt and pain to realize the consequences of unforgiveness that had a root embedded deep in my heart caused from family dysfunction and abandonment. By releasing it all to God, he will work you through it and give you healing. It doesn't mean you have to repair the brokenness of the relationship. But when you release the pain and let the Lord do his work to repair, heal, and restore you, freedom comes to our lives and permeates our hearts with God's love. Giving up our unforgiving iniquities into the hands of our Lord brings the strength and grace needed to heal the wounds that are so deeply embedded into our souls.

Michael Dye writes in his book *The Genesis Process* that early childhood brain development can have a direct influence on what you struggle with later in life.

In the first years of your life (especially the first two), the part of your brain that is developing has to do with your ability to bond, trust, and relate to others. It grows from your experiences with your caregivers and your environment. During this period the brain basically decides whether the world is safe or dangerous. As a baby, you cannot survive on your own. You have to depend on others to have your needs met. If you cry out in need and the need gets met in a comforting way, you will come to believe that having needs that create vulnerability are a good thing because they result in comfort and reward, i.e., the world is safe. Two things happen: 1) you learn to receive gratification from others, and 2) your brain becomes creative and explores the world around you.

But if you are born into a dysfunctional, abusive, or addicted family and your needs don't get met, you will experience the world as unsafe, creating stress. Having needs makes you vulnerable. When crying out results in abuse or neglect, the brain learns that you have to take care of yourself, resulting in what we call a survival, or hyper-vigilant, brain. The brain starts searching for ways to feel normal or free of stress. If you can't bond and trust others, you have to learn to gratify yourself. The brain can begin to actually cut off the neurons that are learning to trust and bond because trying to trust and bond results in pain, fear and stress. This can be the beginning of what predisposes you to become attracted to self-gratifying coping behaviors.

—The Genesis Process
By Michael Dye, CADC, NCAC II

After learning this, I realized that I had a severe lack of trust for people due to multiple abandonment issues from diapers to my teen years. I was unable to bond in a loving relationship and was always eager to bail out. There never was deep contentment or satisfaction because I did not know what it felt like to have my needs met. Contentment was never real and tangible feelings that occurred in my life. I believe that this has had me in bondage since I was a baby. It explains the multiple failed attempts to find love. My coping behaviors were leading me down a destructive, sinful path. But there is hope because God is our Father. He is capable of healing the deep wounds of the brain because the brain connects to the deep things of the heart.

God is a father to the fatherless and to the motherless. You don't receive the spirit of bondage with Father God because you are adopted into the kingdom and heirs with Christ. God never punishes us for the past; remember always that our sins are as far away as the east is from the west. He *forgives* us, but we must repent first. The fervent heart prayer is heard by God when we truly fall to our knees in repentance and ask him to take over our life and live for him. True repentance is when we actually turn away from our rebellious and defiant ways and look to the Lord Jesus for the grace to obey his Word.

It is important for us to forgive everyone in our life who has done things that offend us. To have mercy and forgiveness is not so much for the other person but for you because it sets you free. When you forgive, you are setting yourself free from the anger inside your heart that you hold toward another. An unforgiving heart makes you miserable and unhappy, because when you think about the situation, it stirs tension in your thought life and corrupts your heart. Forgiving doesn't mean you have to always accept what it was that hurt you or to restore a relationship, but it does mean that you consciously and verbally express your release of all hard feelings and give it to God to heal it and take it from you. The freedom brings peace of mind, not for the other person, but for you. The Bible says to hate someone is no different than to have murder in your heart toward them. When we are willing to do what God asks us to do, like forgiving the unforgivable and loving the unlovely, he pours out enough grace that is sufficient. It will change your life, not so much the other person. And by his grace, we can accomplish things that will take you to a new level of trust and closeness to God. He loves us so much and wants us to free our own hearts in order to love others. Grace is poured out on those who ask him. God loves us so much that he wants to give us all good things.

> Be kind and compassionate to one another, forgiving each other, just as in Christ God forgave you.
> Ephesians 4:32 (NIV)

> For if you forgive men when they sin against you, your heavenly Father will also forgive you. But if you do not forgive men their sins, your Father will not forgive your sins.
> Matthew 6:14–15 (NIV)

Then Peter came to Jesus and asked, "Lord, how many times shall I forgive my brother when he sins against me? Up to seven times?"

Matthew 18:21 (NIV)

If he sins against you seven times in a day, and seven times comes back to you and says, "I repent," forgive him.

Luke 17:4 (NIV)

Day Eight

I am not even out of bed, and I had to grab my journal to record what just took place as I was trying to wake up this morning! I was in a sound sleep and was woken up by a bright ray of light that felt like sunshine on my face. It was warm like the sun and bright enough to wake me, because I thought the sun was beaming in my bedroom window. It was so bright I was squinting. I opened my eyes, and there was no sun shining in—the blinds were shut, and the sun does not hit that side of my house, but the opposite side, in the mornings. God's presence was all over me! The light that woke me was brighter than any golden light of a beautiful sunset I have ever seen or experienced. It was a warm flash and had movement to it that moved over my face. As I opened my eyes, I heard God's voice speak to me, and he said, "It's time to get up." *Wow*!

Later today, God revealed to me that my prayers have reached heaven and that Satan is nowhere near me right now! God said his strength will get me through and miracles are taking place in the silent places of my loved ones' hearts. God will lift me up and carry me through for *his* glory! I have crossed through the barriers and into the holy of holies with our Lord. His light is brighter in my soul and my mind than ever before, and his voice calls out to me with clarity.

It was an amazingly blessed day, as the Lord filled me with energy to complete my task and work all day. I have relaxed into a state of calm within my body, and it feels as if my spirit can feel, hear, and see. It is a realm outside fleshly reality. I have a hard time explaining it in my words, but I pray that the Holy Spirit will give me words of wisdom to properly document this journey I call "Into His Light."

Fasting is something people look at as hard, painful, unbearable, or difficult. I've never fasted more than one day in my life. This experience is waking up every part of my soul and teaching me to trust God in such a powerful way. His promises are true and for whosoever will take a hold of them and apply them to their life. God is good and wants to give us all things; and when we sacrifice our whole lives, our minds, and our bodies, he will open up the heavens, and his glory will shine on us.

Praise the Father, the Son, and the Holy Spirit as I enter into day nine!

Day Nine

Indeed, the darkness shall not hide from You, But the night shines as the day; The darkness and the light are both alike to You.

Psalm 139:12 (NKJV)

There is no darkness nor shadow of death where the workers of iniquity may hide themselves.

Job 34:22 (NKJV)

I often pondered how God took me out of such a dark place or why I ever decided to live in darkness. But I am to never look back, because darkness and light are nothing to our Lord—he can take either of them and bring glory to his name!

My darkroom of life in the past was as bright as the noonday to the Lord, and he knew ahead of time where he would have me be at this moment. That is what I call an *awesome God*!

The battle has been letting the flesh go so that the spirit can take control. God's power is present. His presence has given me confidence that he really is in control of all things in my life.

I woke up in a calm state of mind this morning and had to ask the Lord to show up and be with me. I know he is with me, but I prayed, "Oh, God. Show yourself to me, and let my fasting not be in vain. Give me the needed strength daily, and let my efforts honor you! There are those short moments I feel I am in the darkroom of development, but for you, Lord, I know that the darkness is as the light to you. Because you know no darkness, only light. Praise you!"

Night has come, and I am entering day ten! My stomach makes many groans tonight. I am waiting on the Lord to make a move in my life. I am feeling disconnected and a bit detached physically, almost far from my real life in a daily routine. Working seems effortless, no worries, I'm cruising along like on cloud nine; but at the same time, I am wanting a more close connection to God's presence more and more. When I get a glimpse of him, I want more and more! I can't seem to get enough of the Lord's love through all this.

I am learning that to be separated from God is the worst thing that could ever come over me. Lost souls will be in anguish when they die and meet the Lord, only to learn that they will be eternally separated forever from the love of God. One of my assignments from the Lord is to share the gospel! So many people need his love, and I want to open those doors for the lost. My beginning is through sistersofchange.org, a new ministry God has put into my heart. Only God can grow this with the blessing and anointing of the Holy Spirit. I see the vision but must give it all to him because I have no idea how it will begin and where he wants me to take it right now; so I will wait on the Lord. My prayers go up to you, Lord.

Lord, You know my heart. My heart yearns for you. You have removed many negatives from my thoughts, emotions, and habits over these past nine days, and it seems you are turning them into positives. Let me now enter into a new place with you tomorrow.

Day Ten

I was dreaming that I was eating chocolate-covered raisins and I spit them in my hand and threw them on the ground, saying, "I'm fasting!" It sure tasted good in the dream! You think that I would be dreaming about BBQ'd anything with mashed potatoes, veggies, and such. Fasting causes your whole soul, your complete being, and all your thoughts to become fixated on God.

I had to look it up to get the full reason my mind picked that word. The first two are a good description of my love I feel for Jesus and my visual gaze I have upon our Lord.

> Fixate means to make fixed, stationary, or unchanging
> > to focus one's gaze on
> > to direct toward an infantile form of gratification
> > to focus or concentrate one's gaze or attention intently or obsessively
> > > —Miriam-Webster Dictionary

My sleep is restless, and my body aches in every joint clear to the bone marrow. It feels as if my body is pulling blood, fluids, and substance from the depths of my bones to sustain me. I have no idea where I get the energy to work all day like I do. Oh yeah … my strength comes from you, Lord! And again, I quote, "I can do all things through Christ, who strengthens me" (Philippians 4:13, NKJV).

I am at the halfway point in my fast. Twelve hours into the tenth day. That makes ten days and twelve hours to go, then I will finish nineteen days on the Daniel fast to complete my forty days. I lift up my children and family to you, Lord, to be with them today. My family is my rock and my reason for this fast. Jesus is my first rock and my salvation and my hope of all things to come.

The Lord interpreted my dream I had this morning! I remember eating the chocolate-covered raisins. They were creamy, sweet, and melted in my mouth; and when I realized I was eating them, I quickly spit them in my hand and threw them on the ground. The Lord said it represented how sweet and alluring the things of this world can be. If we have a steady diet of the ways of the world (chocolate raisins), it will produce no nutrition or food value (spiritual nourishment), and like the sweet taste of the sugar to the tongue, too much will rot your teeth and cause decay, just as the fruit of the flesh brings ruin, decay, and death. The fruit of the spirit brings us life and life eternal with our Lord! Just as it says in Romans 8:6 (HCSB):"For the mind-set of the flesh is death, but the mind-set of the Spirit is life and peace."

So spitting out the chocolate raisins in my dream represented my true heart desires to keep pressing forward for the things of God. Because the temporary pleasures like taste are just that: temporary! Feed the spirit, and it will wake up and live! Starve the flesh, and it will surely die. "Therefore submit to God. Resist the devil and he will flee from you" (James 4:7, NKJV).

The most important thing to me in this life is to live for Christ so that my light shines for him. He is calling me close to hear his voice; he is going to use me in ways I can't even imagine possible right now. I am learning to be still and listen to the Lord so that in his perfect timing He may use me for His glory.

A year ago, I bought a book titled *Starting a Women's Ministry.* I took it home, and it has sat on the shelf. Every time I looked at it, I would think to myself, *Why did I buy that? What in the world was I thinking?* I had so many thoughts of unworthiness to mentor anyone in the ways of the Lord. But God spoke up and said, "*Read it!*"

He has a plan and a big purpose for me, and my vision for God is to mentor women who specifically feel unworthy, unwanted, insecure, and have low self-esteem. God loves women; we are his royal daughters—daughters of the King Most High! He will teach me, and I pray for his anointing to show his ways and not mine, to share the gospel of Jesus in such a way that will empower everyone who hear his messages of hope. His love and his healing power will give hope to the hopeless so that we can fill the kingdom full of healthy minds for the coming of Jesus Christ.

I am having moments of the reality of my own brokenness of heart and how life has taken its toll on my emotions, beat me down, and left me to the dogs of this world. We live in such a broken world that is in a state of "who cares." Jesus commands us to love not only others and our neighbors, but I believe it goes all the way to our own hearts. We must learn to love ourselves, not in a vain or narcissistic mindset, but in a healthy way that leads us to a healthy self-esteem that will guide us in decisions for life. When we are broken, we can't make a wise decision. We look toward others to fill our needs and our happiness. We look to others to fill that void that only Jesus fills up in us. Brokenness is defined so well, and one of the last definitions is divorce, separation, and desertion or abandonment of a parent—I had all three and more in my life. Brokenness can't be described better than right here in the book of a dictionary:

> Broken:
> Violently separated into parts : shattered
> Damaged or altered by breaking: as having undergone or been subjected to fracture (a broken leg). Being irregular, interrupted, or full of obstacles. Violated by transgression (a broken promise). Discontinuous, interrupted or disrupted by change. Made weak or infirm, Subdued completely: crushed, sorrowful (a broken heart and or a broken spirit). Bankrupt. Reduced in rank. Cut off : disconnected. Not complete or full (a broken bale of hay). Disunited by divorce, separation, or desertion of one parent (children from broken homes and or a broken family). Brokenness.
> —Meriam-Webster Dictionary

I came home from working a long day and found myself crying before the Lord and repenting all the brokenness that has led me to poor decisions and a sinful life. I can never turn back the clock or repair what I did in my past. And my awareness of this has brought me to my knees once again in broken spirit. But Jesus is there to heal all your hurt, pain, and past. He throws our sin as far away as the east is from the west. He wants very much to make us whole again. Brokenness can make you feel hindered in life and unsure of yourself. I know that it made me feel so ordinary and so insignificant. Everyone is significant in God's world! We all have a place he wants us to be—a place where he can mold us and make us all who we were meant to be. When we are so crushed in spirit and broken from deep within our souls, God mourns for us. All we need to do is cry out to him, and he is merciful to save us and heal us.

> The Lord is close to the brokenhearted and saves those who are crushed in spirit. A righteous man may have many troubles, but the Lord delivers him from them all; he protects all his bones, not one of them will be broken.
>
> Psalm 34:18–20 (NIV)

> He heals the brokenhearted and binds up their wounds. He counts the number of the stars; He calls them all by name. Great is our Lord, and mighty is power; His understanding is infinite.
>
> Psalm 147:3–5 (NKJV)

Has our God brought me here to show me something and to give me grace through my darkest times? I believe he has an assignment for me and for everyone reading this. God is never done working within us. He has not put me in the wrong place or the wrong city, or never have I been in a moment that was not in his plan. He knew before I was born where he would have me go and where I would be hurt and wounded and brokenhearted. He also knew the day he would call me to his grace and his healing power. He is my Creator and has me where he wants me right now. His plan for me is to love all and help others know about him, and everyone needs to remember he gives us *his* power to do all things.

> The Spirit of the Sovereign Lord is on me,
>
> Because the Lord has anointed me to preach good news to the poor.
>
> He has sent me to bind up the brokenhearted, to proclaim freedom for the captives and release from darkness for the prisoners, to proclaim the year of the Lord's favor and the day of vengeance of our God, to comfort all who mourn, and provide for those who grieve in Zion—
>
> To bestow on them a crown of beauty instead of ashes,
>
> The oil of gladness instead of mourning,
>
> And a garment of praise instead of a spirit of despair.
>
> They will be called oaks of righteousness, a planting of the Lord for the display of his splendor.
>
> They will rebuild the ancient ruins and restore the places long devastated; they will renew

the ruined cities that have been devastated for generations.

Aliens will shepherd your flocks; foreigners will work your fields and vineyards.

And you will be called priests of the Lord, you will be named ministers of our God.

You will feed on the wealth of nations, and in their riches you will boast.

Instead of their shame my people will receive a double portion and instead of disgrace they will rejoice in their inheritance; and so they will inherit a double portion in their land, and everlasting joy will be theirs.

Isaiah 61:1–7 (NIV)

As the day ends, I am weary and weak, with a hungry stomach. Fasting is a time of mourning and crying. I feel left behind, abandoned, and lonely. I know the Lord is with me and that the brokenness I have gone through today is in his hands. It is hard living alone and coming home every night alone, but my strength and my hope is in Jesus Christ first before any human relationship. It is his love and his presence that keeps my joy and happiness flowing. No person on earth will fill that, but only Christ.

The ever-so-strong presence of God is or at least it seems out of reach for this moment. I pray right now, Holy Spirit come and calm me. Take my pain, and comfort me so I may sleep. Fasting is not fun but a very humbling time before the Lord, giving him my body and ministering to him *for once ... for all!* He is my King, and I will praise him!

Day Eleven

I had a very challenging day. I am weak and growing weary. It was particularly hard to groom today. Hunger is intense, my thirst has increased, and my focus is constantly on the Lord for strength. I need your presence to surround me, Lord. I need your arms to hold me up. My head feels light and buzzes. My heart feels heavy, and I find it hard to pray. My energy is sapped, and it takes effort to just speak or utter words.

My stomach hurts. It growls and pains me. But praise him who so graciously fills me with his strength. He fills my thoughts with his presence. My reasons for sacrifice are greater than my need for food. He will open the gates of heaven for me. He hears the cry of my past and heals all my pain and afflictions. The strongholds that bind my family are being released, and God is in control to dictate the future outcome while I feel angels battling warfare in heaven over me. His power will flow through me, his blessings will fall on me, and all the earth will know his favor and that his mercies have chosen to give me grace and love. Praise the Father, Son, and Holy Spirit.

My life is in your hands, Oh God! "You, O Lord, keep my lamp burning; my God turns my darkness into light" (Psalm 18:28, NIV).

After thoughts

We all know we live by grace, but do we really know what it means to the core? Do we understand the power that Jesus's blood has bestowed over us and the grace he gave us so we could approach our Father in heaven as white as snow and with boldness? Grace is an amazing, wonderful gift—just like the song "Amazing Grace" sings.

Grace is unmerited favor from God. Good things that are not deserved, especially salvation! Grace is sufficiency. The dictionary has a very good description of grace. It is powerfully put:

> It is unmerited divine assistance given to humans for their regeneration or sanctification.
>
> A virtue coming from God; a state of sanctification enjoyed through divine grace.
>
> It is complete approval and favor, mercy, and pardon.
>
> Disposition to or an act or instance of kindness, courtesy, or clemency
>
> —Merriam-Webster Dictionary

> For the Lord God is a sun and shield; the Lord bestows favor and honor; no good thing does he withhold from those whose walk is blameless.
>
> Psalm 84:11 (NIV)

I always thank God for you because of his grace given you in Christ Jesus.

1 Corinthians 1:4 (NIV)

Concerning this salvation, the prophets, who spoke of the grace that was to come to you, searched intently and with the greatest care,

1 Peter 1:10 (NIV)

In order that in the coming ages he might show the incomparable riches of his grace, expressed in his kindness to us in Christ Jesus.

Ephesians 2:7 (NIV)

To the praise of His glorious grace that He favored us with in the Beloved. In Him we have redemption through His blood, the forgiveness of our trespasses, according to the riches of His grace that He lavished on us with all wisdom and understanding. He made known to us the mystery of His will, according to His good pleasure that He planned in Him for the administration of the days of fulfillment to bring everything together in the Messiah, both things in heaven and things on earth in Him. In Him we were also made His inheritance, predestined according to the purpose of the One who works out everything in agreement with the decision of His will.

Ephesians 1:6–11 (HCSB)

To that, just as sin reigned in death, so also grace might reign through righteousness to bring eternal life through Jesus Christ our Lord.

Romans 5:21 (NIV)

And they will pray for you with deep affection because of the overflowing grace God has given to you. Thank God for this gift too wonderful for words!

2 Corinthians 9:14–15 (NLT)

But He said to me, "My grace is sufficient for you, for power is perfected in weakness."

Therefore, I will most gladly boast all the more about my weaknesses, so that Christ's power may reside in me.

2 Corinthians 12:9 (HCSB)

But the gift is not like the trespass. For if the many died by the trespass of the one man, how much more did God's grace and the gift that came by the grace of the one man, Jesus Christ, overflow to the many! Again, the gift of God is not like the result of the one man's sin: The judgment followed one sin and brought condemnation, but the gift followed many trespasses and brought justification. For if, by the trespass of the one man, death reigned through that one man, how much more will those who receive God's abundant provision of grace and of the gift of righteousness reign in life through the one man, Jesus Christ.

Romans 5:15–17 (NIV)

And now I entrust you to God and the message of his grace that is able to build you up and give you an inheritance with all those he has set apart for himself.

Acts 20:32 (NLT)

But even before I was born, God chose me and called me by his marvelous grace. Then it pleased him.

Galatians 1:15 (NLT)

Being justified freely by His grace through the redemption that is in Christ Jesus,

Romans 3:24 (NKJV)

Whom he poured out on us generously through Jesus Christ our Savior, so that, having been justified by his grace, we might become heirs having the hope of eternal life.

Titus 3:6–7 (NIV)

But he said to me, "My grace is sufficient for you, for my power is made perfect in weakness." Therefore I will boast all the more gladly about my weaknesses, so that Christ's power may rest on me.

2 Corinthians 12:9 (NIV)

God's grace is our only source of strength in this broken and corrupt world. His love and his grace will cover your life with protection and strength to endure whatever you bring to the throne. In Christ, we are strong; without Christ, we can do nothing. His power and his grace are truly sufficient in all our weaknesses. We must remember that if we have faith in him, we have faith in *all* things.

It takes strength and faith to place your life completely in His hands every single day and trust Him to direct your path. He will never give us more than we can handle.

Even if we endure pain, suffering, heartache, or joy, it does not matter if our day is happy or sad because our Lord's grace is sufficient in all things.

> But because of his great love for us, God, who is rich in mercy, made us alive with Christ even when we were dead in transgressions, it is by grace you have been saved. And God raised us up with Christ and seated us with him in the heavenly realms in Christ Jesus, in order that in the coming ages he might show the incomparable riches of his grace, expressed in his kindness to us in Christ Jesus. For it is by grace you have been saved, through faith and this not from yourselves, it is the gift of God.
>
> Ephesians 2:4–8 (NIV)

The day you give your heart to Christ, an amazing transformation takes place from the inside out. We are born with sin and live in sin, and sin will destroy us if we do not repent to God and ask Christ to come into our hearts.

When he comes in, we suddenly become alive. That is amazing grace that only comes from the Father.

Our Father in heaven takes us up as righteous and can now accept us as his children. If you can visualize God picking you up and putting you in a seat next to him and all he sees is Jesus and the blood of salvation over you, then you are seeing the truth and the promise that is given to us through Christ. He sees no sin in you when you are covered by the blood. There is nothing we can do to earn this right to sit in heavenly places with Jesus. It is God's kindness given to us, and he forgives us through faith in

Jesus Christ. We are saved only by that faith and not by any other thing that we could do. It is a free gift, and we need to take a hold of it and cling to it and accept it as our promised inheritance. Praise Jesus Christ for his grace and his blood over our lives!

> May Jesus himself and God our Father, who reached out in love and surprised you with gifts of unending help and confidence, put a fresh heart in you, invigorate your work, enliven your speech.
> 2 Thessalonians 2:16 (The Message)

We need to rejoice and be filled with his joy every day because of his unending love. It is the gifts and unending help we receive from the Father that give us an eternal confidence. It is this refreshing eternal love that builds a brand new heart into every new believer. It gives us a reason to live and to be the best we can be in all we do, from our relationships to the work place. It is a love the Father bestows on us that even causes our speech and our thought life to change. His love turns our hearts and our very life inside out, and he uses everything we were and everything we are becoming for his glory!

Day Twelve

The Holy Spirit has been with me through these few days of fasting, and I have been taken down to a level of repentance that has revealed so many of my past conditions and my brokenness, and he is revealing to me that he is healing me and transforming everything for his glory.

I woke up this morning, and you are here with me. I get up, and you get up with me. I go to work, and you work all around me. I come home and collapse, and you are there to comfort me.

This morning, I knew you were inside me—in my sleeping, and in my waking up. You follow me in my coming and going. I am realizing you are the very breath of life, Jehovah Jira, my provider. Your promises are for *whosoever*, as it says so in John 3:16 (NIV): "For God so loved the world that he gave his one and only Son, that whoever believes in him shall not perish but have eternal life."

I am a descendent of Abraham. Just one of those grains of sand in the big scheme of things to come. God's provision is here and now, and he is coming soon. He will give me all I could ever hope for or ask for and can even imagine.

> Now to him who is able to do immeasurably more than all we ask or imagine, according to his power that is at work within us, to him be glory in the church and in Christ Jesus throughout all generations, for ever and ever! Amen.
>
> Ephesians 3:20–21 (NIV)

As I press on for today, his love will get me through into tomorrow. The time draws nearer to the finish line. I can do all things through Christ, who strengthens me! I say that over and over all day long! Speak the Word out loud into your life daily; it gives power and strength to your day.

I have only ten days to go. I fight the battle of a painful stomach and draw my strength and power from God, who gives generously to anyone who asks. I have become bold and confident in approaching the throne of God to lay down and submit my request before him. Through my fast, I have gained insight and have learned what temptation really feels like to the core of my whole being and from the deep parts of my stomach. But instead, I go to the throne of grace. Because, "In him and through faith in him we may approach God with freedom and confidence" (Ephesians 3:12).

In all of life, when we are tempted, we first have the desire, then our minds talk us into it until we give way to its power to give in to the temptation. I have learned that if I can fast twelve days, walk through a grocery store for only broth, cook a big breakfast for eight girls and not nibble, then I can most certainly resist any temptation that this world would throw at me. Fasting and that starvation feeling of the flesh is the most difficult thing I have ever had to overcome. Eating is such a pleasure, such a gift from God that when you abstain from it, you feel the mourning, the pain, and the suffering that much of the world feels every day on this earth. It is the time to take all of your pain to prayer. It has broken bad habits in me and shown me the true meaning of killing the flesh so that the spirit can commune with our Lord.

> No temptation has seized you except what is common to man. And God is faithful; he will not let you be tempted beyond what you can bear. But when you are tempted, he will also provide a way out so that you can stand up under it.
> 1 Corinthians 10:13 (NIV)

As believers in Jesus Christ, we need to take hold of Scripture and the promises he has for us and apply it to our lives—believing the very truth and Word of God. God is sovereign. Praise him forever. Bless his holy name, and all honor goes to Jesus, who shed his blood for us.

My journey is to gain knowledge and to know what God's will is for my life. I want to know of the things he planned for me long ago that I did not complete and to know if my visions for speaking and sharing my testimony are his true calling for my life and not just some cooked-up idea that has entered my head. God is faithful, as he laid my heart on this scripture.

The Message Bible states it like this, in 1 Thessalonians 5:24: "The One who called you is completely dependable. If he said it, he'll do it!"

I know in my heart he has called me; however, I pray and lean on his Word to guide me and help me do his will and not mine. This is powerful because I am not worthy of my own efforts and knowledge but only able to complete his assignment, if he anoints it with the Holy Spirit and that it is his complete and glorious will. He will make the way. He will bring it to pass by his power only and through my willingness to obey. I am his, even though I have faults and fears. He will strengthen my every weakness.

As this day closes, I am entering into another day closer to my Lord. Each day draws me near. Each day is different from the one before. I pray for more grace. Please pour it over me generously, Lord. Hunger has turned a bit painful, but my fight to the finish line for my Lord is more important. I am very serious in my prayer request before you, Lord. I am in expectation of answered prayer, blessings, breakthroughs, and salvation for all my family. I wait to see miracles in my life, in my family, and in my finances and in all areas God has planned for me long ago. I love you, Lord; you are my only provider. Let your will be done!

As I close this day, he has revealed to me that he is light. He has heard my prayers, and it is a total submission to him who provides for me. It shows me how much I need God and how weak I am without him. Being hungry *hurts*, but *his* spiritual food satisfies and fulfills my soul to its core.

Father, I pray that you send me a helpmate—a life partner, the one you would choose for me. I will not settle for anything less than the one whom you send and who loves you first.

Father, let your will take precedence in my life.

Day Thirteen

I must continually pray and seek him so that I will receive grace to get through another day! Father, I send up my prayers for our youth today, for salvation. Give power and protect those who love you in all the earth that face terrible persecution or death. Give them grace, and be with them. I thank you, Lord, that I live in a place where I don't have to worry right now about that kind of threat because I believe in you. I am having a heavy heart today for the body of Christ across the world.

> Give in to God, come to terms with him and everything will turn out just fine. Let him tell you what to do; take his words to heart. Come back to God Almighty and he'll rebuild your life. Clean house of everything evil. Relax your grip on your money and abandon your gold-plated luxury. God Almighty will be your treasure, more wealth than you can imagine.
>
> You'll take delight in God, the Mighty One, and look to him joyfully, boldly. You'll pray to

him and he'll listen; he'll help you do what you've promised. You'll decide what you want and it will happen; your life will be bathed in light. To those who feel low you'll say, 'Chin up! Be brave!' and God will save them. Yes, even the guilty will escape, escape through God's grace in your life."

Job 22:21–30 (The Message)

I must remind myself daily my reasons for fasting. It is for my family—for salvation, restoration, and for God to give back to me the years I lost due to my own poor decisions without him. I pray for complete and total repair. I pray for life to be restored back to me like it was in the days of my youth. Restoration shall be given back to me in a double portion, with God's blessings. I see God's love, grace, and mercy falling upon my family. I see my children's children praising the Lord! I see my children looking upon their father in awe and wonder—with love and praise to God, the Father of fathers, for such restored miracles. Praise you, Lord, for your Word. It uplifts me, teaches me, and guides me to truth and understanding. You are amazing, all powerful, and omnipresent. I love you, Lord Jesus. Be with me today, and pour out your grace that gives me strength.

I was talking with a dear friend in Christ today, and our conversation arose on the subject of a true woman's role for Christ concerning relationships with men or husbands. Women have been under the attack of Satan now for years. In the 1960s, a shift occurred—women's rights and society were teaching that women were able to dominate men and that they should feel equal or even stronger emotionally than men and thus developed the independent woman. Women have, for a long time, been under the stronghold of the so-called "liberated" independent and in-need-of-no-help-from-man syndrome since the '60s. It has totally removed the word *respect* for our counter partner, the man. Women have become selfish and expect men to respect them when it needs to start the other way around. Some of you women may not agree, but it is so in the Bible. I am not saying that we should become a doormat for men to walk on, but our role as women need to get back to biblical understanding of who we are in Christ.

Most men are in such need of a woman who will respect him and love him the way God intended. Be the helpmate and the best friend without judgment, belittlement, or perfection expectation. We are all guilty of that and need to ask God to restore women to be strong in the areas of life that really make a difference in the kingdom of God and not what the world thinks. Our society today has become fixed on selfishness, self-centeredness, and the "what-about-me attitude." There is no man or woman on the planet that will make you "happy" or "content" until you find that love, joy, and happiness that comes from God first. God calls us to love one another, to serve one another no matter what we think, feel, or see. He wants our love to be first focused on him and him only. Love Jesus and the Father first and foremost. Jesus's words are in all four Gospels on this matter: Seek the kingdom of God above all else, and he will give you everything you need (Luke 12:31). Respect your man, and treat your woman right. All things will be given to the relationship that is flourishing and satisfying.

> But seek first his kingdom and his righteousness, and all these things will be given to you as well. Therefore do not worry about tomorrow, for tomorrow will worry about itself. Each day has enough trouble of its own.
>
> Matthew 6:33 (NIV)

If we want good things, good relationships, good health, and blessings, then we must first submit to God all of our being. No thing (nothing) or no person will ever fulfill our needs, only God. That was the big mistake in my own life! I expected people to make me happy, relationships to fix all my loneliness, and money to have all the things we think make us more complete. It's all a lie from the enemy.

As I close this day and move into day fourteen, I will praise and thank the Lord for his grace that has gotten me this far. May this psalm rest in your soul. Ponder each word, and praise our Father for the Word: our Bible.

> Deep calls to deep in the roar of your waterfalls;
> All your waves and breakers have swept over me.
>   By day the Lord directs his love, at night his song is with me-a prayer to the God of my life.
>
> Psalm 42:7–8 (NIV)

Day Fourteen

Father! *Lord*! *Jesus*! Thank you and praise you for bringing me this far. My worship has changed in all areas of my life, especially learning to be a living and walking, breathing sacrifice for your glory, Lord. Thank you, and all praise be to you.

I feel good physically today—better than any day yet! The Lord's presence is strong, penetrating, and real. I am looking forward to worship at church this morning. Praise you, Father!

> Now faith is being sure of what we hope for and certain of what we do not see.
>
> Hebrews 11:1 (NIV)

We are learning in church a new series on being fruitful for the Lord. This is a thought-provoking note I recorded in my church journal notes, and it still resonates deep within my very soul.

> Fruitful: one who is implanted and abiding in Christ; growing, increasing, abounding, flourishing, and reproducing much fruit.
>
> —Personal Notes

Lord, I want to be fruitful in my walk with you always. I want to abide in you and you in me. I have a great need to be continually connected to you. You are truly the "I AM."

Today ended well. I went to fellowship with friends at a potluck dinner with my dear group of singles from my past church. I had soup, of course; nothing in it, just liquid. I did awesome around all the food and realized how good the Lord really is and how much he really loves me. Seven days left, and then I begin to eat lightly with the Daniel fast. Every minute of every day, God, is in my face, present in my heart, and speaking to me his Glory and his will that will be taking place through my life. He is awesome! My spirit has tuned into God's airwaves completely and has been the most satisfying spiritual experience a human can have. It has been just like taking a huge glimpse into eternity with him. Life here is only a vapor, a mist. His presence reminds me of why I am fasting. My worship has gained a seriousness of joy and pleasure, bringing him glory and honor, and I have developed a true desire and longing for God to take notice of my prayers. I have been battling spiritual warfare and knowing all along the way that I am winning. Matter of fact, I am sure by now I have totally and completely pissed off the devil. I have been given authority and power over all of Satan's strongholds, and he cannot injure my family or me anymore.

Victory is ahead for me. Miracles are taking place in the heavens while God's servant angels are doing my bidding and ministering to me as I offer up all that I am, all that I do, and all that I have to him who loves me. Praise him!

Day Fifteen

I am almost too weak to write. Work was hard, my emotions are high, and my defenses are weakened by the craving to eat. God has given me much grace for making it this far. I feel the Holy Spirit's strength and see the end in sight. My mind is empty, as my stomach and the cares of what's going on in the world have left my thoughts.

I was worried I would not finish this fast, but after the first few days, his grace took over. I know all my prayers have reached the heavens. It has been an irreplaceable experience that has opened a door to God that I never want to close.

I pray tonight, Father, that you anoint my gifts so that I understand what my personal and spiritual assigned task are so that you may send me out into the kingdom to help you harvest souls. Let me give *you* glory, and never let what I do be for my gain but done for *you*. Bless me indeed with your gifts, expand my horizons, and keep your hand on me so that evil is far from me.

I need to rest not only my body but also my soul tonight. Less than one week to go.

G'night, precious Lord. I love you.

Day Sixteen

This has broken my flesh in two and shows me that my body is *his* temple where the Holy Spirit dwells. I will fill it with only good things of the Lord. Father, the one reason for my fast is for you to reveal my assignment in ministry for you. Show me, speak to me, and give me direction. Bless me, expand my territory, and keep your hand on me, and keep me from evil!

I woke up this morning with two clear visions. The first was a head of a cow, like a young calf, and it had a cloud-like cover or foamy-looking cap on its head. It was just sitting on top of the cow's head, circular in shape and flat. The color of it was black. The Lord said that the black covering over the cow represented darkness, and the stronghold of Satan and the cow is an idol. His message to me was that my family is protected from the world's polluted religious idols and false gods (or false religious beliefs). My prayers for my family's salvation has been heard in the heavens, and God said they are all safe—protected also from being deceived in these last days as we know them.

The second vision was a round table with a cloth over it, and a cup with no handle on it was in the middle of the table. The cup had a lot of pens in it. The Lord spoke to me and said, "Keep writing."

The day is ending, and I am moving into day seventeen. I had a thicker soup tonight, butternut squash. It did not sit well with my tummy. I am going to have to try and slowly bring the fast down to food by Sunday. It is very hard to sleep through the nights because of hunger. My prayers are fervent and constant, even though I am weak. I fall into bed and cry because my mind is not focused on normal life but only on my life in eternity, and what I do here and now will affect eternal things. God is very present, and I am so connected to a different realm right now. All I think about is sending up my prayers every day. My walk with the Lord is the only thing that matters at this moment.

My body is cold from lack of food. Tomorrow will be here faster than I know it. One more day to work through fasting. "I can do all things through Christ, who strengthens me" (Philippians 4:13, NKJV).

Day Seventeen

I had a good day. I feel amazingly healthy; however, my focus is scattered when it comes to business. It takes effort to concentrate. I caught my thoughts this morning, questioning my fast and if it is in vain or if God really hears my cries in prayer. Satan is the father of lies! I am really squashing him (Satan) under my feet, and he is afraid of me now—but mostly, pissed off. I will not worry. I will trust that God is in control of my life, and I must allow him to guide me through all my daily challenges. I need to give him my spirit, along with my body, as I continue this fast.

I am tired a lot and am fighting cold hands and feet. I am praying also for strength and desire, Lord, to go to this retreat at the beach with friends. Please give me strength. What I would really rather do is just stay home, where all is quiet with you, Lord, but it might be best for me to go so that I can minister to someone else's needs and take the focus off of me.

And do not give the devil an opportunity.

Ephesians 4:27 (NASB)

For our struggle is not against flesh and blood, but against the rulers, against the powers, against the world forces of this darkness, against the spiritual forces of wickedness in the heavenly places. Therefore, take up the full armor of God, so that you will be able to resist in the evil day, and having done everything, to stand firm.

Ephesians 6:12–13 (NASB)

Day Eighteen

A day of rest! Praise him! I am doing nothing, except seeking, speaking, and listening to the Lord. I am on the path of golden bricks and breakthroughs. I see the end is near. Better is the end of something than the beginning. It shows completion to a task from my soul and takes me to the crossroads where I will choose to fast another twenty-one days on the Daniel diet. God is so good. I made it to the end! It was a good fight, and it really broke Satan's power over me. God's presence and his hand has been on me like never before in my entire life.

I will see good things happen among the living because of my steadfast diligence. God's test to the fullest was in the grace he bestowed over me in times of physical and emotional weakness, as well as spiritual brokenness. His presence has strengthened me, and my walk with him feels like he is next to me—penetrating my whole body, soul, and mind physically, spiritually, and emotionally. Nothing can hurt me, and no one can hurt me because he loves me and is with me until the end of my earthly journey. Praise him when I get to meet him face-to-face, and praise him while I wait.

> I would have lost heart, unless I had believed that I would see the goodness of the Lord in the land of the living.
>
> Psalm 27:13 (NKJV)

> I will not die, but live, and tell of the works of the Lord. The Lord has disciplined me severely, but He has not given me over to death.
>
> Psalm 118:17–18 (NASB)

> Wait on the Lord; Be of good courage, and He shall strengthen your heart; Wait, I say, on the Lord!
>
> Psalm 27:14 (NKJV)

Day Nineteen

Even though I approach the end of my no-food fasting journey, it feels as if the last few days are longer than the past eighteen. I have today and tomorrow, but God tells me over and over to only take one day at a time. I ask for grace, Lord! This time with you, Lord, has forever changed my walk with you. To describe your love and your presence is only within my heart as I went through transformation. Your love for me has become vivid and alive and in full color. It was like stepping from black-and-white scenes and lifestyles right into a new realm that was in full color and digital clarity, with colors I have never seen before. The sound of your voice has gone from monolog to stereo in my life, from one speaker into surround sound! It penetrates my soul and fills my heart with an everlasting joy—joy like I saw on the morning of day eight. Your brightness filled my room. It was so bright that I could not look into it completely but only had to squint my eyes to bear the view that was over me. The brightness filled my room as your light moved across my face with warmth, love, and much motion. I opened my eyes, and it was gone in the split second, but you left the permanent imprint of your love and presence on my heart and in my room.

My days of fasting and yearning for you have been filled with living food I could have never experienced with an effort to move forward in your grace. The sacrifice does not compare to the returns of grace, love, mercy, and answered prayer that you bestowed on me. I am living in great expectation of all your promises because you have revealed to me that they are true, and your power is in me. Yes, the Lord's promises stand true.

Lord, crush everything in me that hinders and keeps me from serving you completely and being a righteous witness to the world. "Let us hold fast the confession of our hope without wavering, for He who promised is faithful" (Hebrews 10:23, NASB).

Father, I pray for revival this very day to break out over your people, among the very ones I prayed for. Let salvation pour over them as you show mercy and love to my family. Let my prayers ascend into the heavens, like a sweet fragrant aroma that is pleasing to you. Break the years of bondage over my family, and set them *free*! Be my provider, Lord, and my rock forever. Bless your name, Lord, and praise you forever. For you have heard my prayers and have come to deliver me.

> Every part of Scripture is God-breathed and useful one way or another, showing us truth, exposing our rebellion, correcting our mistakes, train-

ing us to live God's way. Through the Word we are put together and shaped up for the tasks God has for us.

2 Timothy 3:16–17 (The Message)

Day Twenty

Today I woke up rested from a hard crash yesterday. I am growing weak and need rest. God's grace is with me, but my body is giving up to lack of energy to keep up the pace. My time will still go on with the Lord as I transition into the well-known diet that Daniel ate before the kings. Fruits, vegetables, whole grains—like lentils, beans, and sprouts— and any thing that comes from the earth. God is good. We are so precious to our Lord, Jesus. He wants to do for us all that we ask for, but he also wants our whole heart in the process. I have given my heart, soul, and body to him who has strengthened me over these past twenty days. I know my prayers are heard and are on their way back to me answered!

> You'll no longer be so full of questions. This is what I want you to do: Ask the Father for whatever is in keeping with the things I've revealed to you. Ask in my name, according to my will, and he'll most certainly give it to you. Your joy will be a river overflowing its banks!
>
> John 16:23–24 (The Message)

His love and miracles are manifesting as I wait in expectancy. His power has been released in all my tears and prayers as I cried out in desperate need for Jesus to be with me. I am nothing without the Lord in my life. All we do on earth is meaningless unless we have the love of the Father in us and Jesus's blood over us.

My visions and assignment from God is to share the gospel on a larger scale than my mind can think or imagine right now, but I believe in what he has placed in my heart. I will take hold of God's Word and have faith enough to apply it to my life and run with it right into his arms of grace and power to do all he asks of me.

> But my life is worth nothing to me unless I use it for finishing the work assigned me by the Lord Jesus, the work of telling others the Good News about the wonderful grace of God.
>
> Acts 20:24 (NLT)

We must learn to walk in freedom and know Christ loves us no matter what. Worship him with an open heart that knows we have been bought by his blood, with all rights to freely approach God with our request without condemnation or worries. God has already approved of us through Jesus, and we need to walk in that freedom. We also need to know the difference between just being saved (accepting Jesus and guaranteed to be a citizen of heaven) and the process of sanctification. Sanctification is a lifelong process of change through the Word of God, the Holy Spirit, and learning to walk out our salvation—with Jesus right by our side. He wants obedience. If we love him, we will obey him. "Those who accept my commandments and obey them are the ones who love me" (John 14:21, NLT).

> Let us then approach the throne of grace with confidence, so that we may receive mercy and find grace to help us in our time of need.
>
> Hebrews 4:16 (NIV)

> So let us come boldly to the throne of our gracious God. There we will receive his mercy, and we will find grace to help us when we need it most.
>
> Hebrews 4:16 (NLT)

As I begin the Daniel fast and come into the privilege of eating once again, I will always remember the sacrifice, the hunger, and the changes that took place in my spirit. My stomach hurts tonight from the food that I put in it. I thought hunger hurt! Food is hurting me worse, and I should have started with soup or a smoothie. Reintroducing food hurts more than abstaining from food. However much it hurts, my energy is back from one meal.

As I realize how wonderfully made we are by God, I know now that I must not defile my body, the temple of the Holy Spirit. Junk food is not going to be a part of my life. Poor health is from practicing bad eating habits, which really is sin. God has removed so many bad habits during my fast that involved things that go in my mouth. I pray that my health will spring forth into a new beginning!

I checked my mail today and was shocked, actually astounded, that I found a beautiful card from my son and his wife. They were amazed I did my fasting in faith. They were touched by God by watching my faithfulness and included a check for $500. All I could do is sob and cry and realize that it was God who touched them and me. That is not a coincidence; this is a direct message from God that he is in control of all things, and he is my provider. Prayers are also being answered in the area of family restoration for my kids, for me, and all I prayed for. My prayers have reached the altar of God in heaven and are presented at the feet of Jesus, delivered by the holy angels who do his bidding. Even though I cannot see results yet, I know they are on their way!

Oh God in heaven, I pray for relief of my stomach tonight. It hurts.

Day Twenty-One

Today I woke up with an uneasy feeling inside me from the food. Digestion is just not happening very well for me right now. I recommend to anyone who is coming off a long fast to start slower than I did. Eat light. I am focusing on soups, smoothies, fruit, and anything soft and easy to digest. Stay away from breads, grains, dairy, and meat for a week or two.

I did have my special time with the Lord through those fasting days, and his presence is all over me. I have nineteen days left to adjust to eating again, but this part of my fast is lifted up to the Lord as a promise to not defile my body with junk. The way most people eat is a sin to this awesome temple God has provided for us. I am not saying you can't ever enjoy something good, eat desserts, or have that great cup of coffee, but what I have learned from the Lord is to care for our temple carefully and mindfully by keeping the indulgent eating to a minimal occasion. Praise him!

Tonight's dinner consisted of broccoli and cooked fresh beets. Mornings, I take my fill of fruit and whole oats.

Lord, help me keep my focus as I diligently become aware of taking care of your temple. I am your creation; you know my needs, my every heartbeat, and all my little aches and pains as my body prepares for excellent changes in health for you. I offer up my whole life, as I know you will provide for me the proper prosperity and health you promise me. "Dear friend, I pray that you may enjoy good health and that all may go well with you, even as your soul is getting along well" (3 John 2, NIV).

The first thing I want to prosper is my mind for Christ. Prosperity is eternal gain, salvation! God knows we have needs, but the first thing to prosper should be the inside of me, which is my soul, my mind, and all my thinking.

Day Twenty-Two

Praise you, Father, for giving me another day here on planet Earth. I still feel the gut wrenching going on in my tummy. I am asking and believing for my health to spring forth and all healing to take place. Your grace and mercy abound; my weakness is made strong because of you. Be with me tomorrow as I work. I still wait on you, Lord. Use me and place me in the right places with the right people. I know you are with me.

God wants to use all of us for specific assignments, but we need to be available. If we are not open at all times and ready for his service, he will pass us by (for the moment) and go find the most available spiritually hungry person to do his assignment, making you wait for his will for the next time around. We must be available, awake, and sensitive to the spirit of God. God wants to bless us all, but we need to learn to be still, be quiet sometimes, and listen to his voice. I ask myself today, is my spirit submitted to him? When we submit ourselves to the spirit, everything seems to work together for the good.

The soul that submits to all of God's disciplines is the soul who truly loves God. Love believes and hopes in all the good things of the Lord. God's love never fails me. His enduring love rests peacefully in my heart because no matter what comes at me in the world, I have his assurance and protection to get me through anything, and that gives me peace.

> Love is patient, love is kind and is not jealous; love does not brag and is not arrogant, does not act unbecomingly; it does not seek its own, is not provoked, does not take into account a wrong suffered, does not rejoice in unrighteousness, but rejoices with the truth; bears all things, believes all things, hopes all things, endures all things. Love never fails.
>
> 1 Corinthians 13:4–8 (NASB)

As long as we focus on the Lord and our desire is to please our Creator, then he will not deprive us of our daily needs. He wants to bless us with his comfort and provisions. He will satisfy the hungry with all his good things, while the rich go away empty. No matter how rich people are, they will feel empty because they do not know him. Everyone who seeks Jesus with all their heart and all their soul will be filled to the full or never be without because his provision is a promise. He satisfies to the fullest inside the soul with spiritual food and the water of life.

Praise You, Lord!

Day Twenty-Three

Praise you, Father. I am starting to know now that when you formed me in my mother's womb, you knew my days and destiny before I was even born. We read it, we know it is true, but I am feeling its truths deep down in my soul— that real knowledge of God's hand on my life.

> For You formed my inward parts; You wove me in my mother's womb. I will give thanks to You, for I am fearfully and wonderfully made; Wonderful are Your works, and my soul knows it very well. My frame was not hidden from You, when I was made in secret, and skillfully wrought in the depths of the earth; your eyes have seen my unformed substance; and in Your book were all written the days that were ordained for me, when as yet there was not one of them.
>
> Psalm 139:13–16 (NASB)

I am in control of *nothing*. Looking back on all the past mistakes I made only holds me back from God's plan for my life. I will press on forward because it is what he wants. It is what he requires so that we can listen to his voice, and if you listen, then you will actually hear God's voice.

Peace with God for me is to make sure that everything I do while in the body here on earth pleases my Lord. That is real peace—knowing he is happy with what I am doing at all times.

> To give light to those who sit in darkness and the shadow of death, to guide our feet into the way of peace.
>
> Luke 1:79 (NKJV)

> Shining on those in the darkness, those sitting in the shadow of death, then showing us the way, one foot at a time, down the path of peace.
>
> Luke 1:79 (The Message)

After thoughts

Healing comes to all who turn to Christ. The definition states clearly how the Lord heals us. By his wounds, we *are* healed.

> The word *heal* is to make sound or whole (heal a wound) to restore to health: to cause (an undesirable condition) to be overcome : mend or to patch up (a breach or division) (heal a breach between friends) to restore to original purity or integrity (healed of sin) to return to a sound state.
>
> —*M-W Collegiate Dictionary* (11th Ed.)

Let's examine each point made in the dictionary about healing. It is knowledge of truth that sets us free indeed.

Then you will know the truth, and the truth will set you free (John 8:32, NIV).

1. We become a new creature in Christ; he heals our mind and emotions, and we begin to know what it means to be complete and whole in Christ.

2. He restores to us our spiritual health that we lost long ago in the garden, where Adam and Eve destroyed their healthy relationship God had in place for them.

3. Jesus gives us the power to overcome our fears, hurts, and past offenses, even though we will always remember them. He gives us strength and power to overcome all things if we remain in his love.

4. The power of forgiveness to patch up means to fix the wrongs that we have done or the wrong others have done to us, giving us the power to move forward in life and learn to love like Christ loves us.

I love these definitions, as they tell us that Christ restores us to our original purity and integrity. Wow. That means we are washed white as snow; all shame, guilt, and sin are gone, and we have a complete and fresh start in our new life with Christ. Actually, his mercies are new every morning. We are healed of our sins every day for the rest of our lives by *grace*. This does not mean it is a license to keep sinning, but it does tell us that Christ renews us and heals us every day until he comes back for us.

Day Twenty-Four

As my days move into a more settled energy from eating, I am praising you, God, even though I sometimes don't feel like you are as near or as close with me like you were through the first half of my journey. Your presence was so very evident and strong. Please do not hide yourself from me, Lord. I believe you are near, always near. You are breaking barriers and walls down that otherwise would have still been there. The strongholds are releasing and dropping off, like dust under my feet!

When I came off the fast into the Daniel diet, I had extreme bowel pain when the food hit my system. I could not get my system to digest and process things for three days. I prayed to God and asked why. Usually fasting will spring forth your health speedily, but I felt just the opposite. Then I learned that for however long you fast, you should take that long to slowly eat again, and I ate too much too soon. As time goes on, I know I will feel better. But I feel as if I have obstructions in my bowels—it's only the food. So my advice to those who fast is to slowly feed yourself.

Since 2003, I have had an ovary issue that plagues me now and then—causing swelling, pain, and discomfort from cysts. That is most of the bowel obstruction I feel from time to time, but please, Lord, not now. It causes back pain, a horrible bloated feeling, and burning sensation throughout my lower abdomen. It has been months since I have had any problems until I ended this fast. I now am dealing with that feeling of being all plugged up inside, without the ability to eliminate my food. All day I have been claiming Psalm 118:17 (NIV), "I will not die but live, and will proclaim what the Lord has done," and also reminding myself that by his stripes, I have been healed. Amen.

I agree with the Word of God that he is my healer and performs the greatness of knitting me back to normal.

> Surely he took up our infirmities and carried our sorrows, yet we considered him stricken by God, smitten by him, and afflicted. But he was pierced for our transgressions, he was crushed for our iniquities; the punishment that brought us peace was upon him, and by his wounds we are healed. We all, like sheep, have gone astray, each of us has turned to his own way; and the Lord has laid on him the iniquity of us all.
>
> Isaiah 53:4–6 (NIV)

I sat down to write more in my journal and caught the last half of the 700 *Club*, and at the end of the program, Pat and Terry always pray for the sick, the lost, etc., and right in the middle of the words of knowledge, Pat Robinson spoke out that "someone has a bowel obstruction, and God is healing that right now." I cried out loudly to the Lord,

"Praise God!" I accept that as *my* healing! Because I have had ovarian problems going on inside me, obstructing my lower bowel for several years after having an ultrasound that showed two golf ball-sized cysts. Pat said the Lord is healing that right now! Of all times in my life, this has been the time I have really experienced God's touch, his presence, and numerous blessings so far since I gave him all of me. I am available and completely devoted to you, Lord, to turn me inside out for your work and for the kingdom. His miracles are still at work in modern day 2008, just the same as it was when Jesus walked the earth. People just don't want to see or believe in miracles anymore, it seems. Jesus gave us power, and that power comes from faith and from speaking the Word of God out loud over our lives.

Praise you, Father, forever and ever! You are good, and you are faithful.

Today was a chilly day for June. I had a nice fire tonight in my fireplace as I finished out my whole evening writing and searching out scripture. It came to my mind that I have not watched any TV until today's 700 *Club* program. I have no desire anymore to fill my mind with the garbage that is in our media today. TV will pollute the mind if you put the wrong stuff in front of your eyes and ears. It affects all who watch too much television. God wants our full attention on him, not on the carnal lust of all the world's goods. TV is all about get this, buy that, eat this, eat that, sexually suggestive programming, violence, and fornication portrayed as romantic, beautiful love affairs. I detest how the media promotes adultery—they just call it multiple relationships outside of marriage or married couples having affairs. It's all about accepting the immoral acts of the world. The world views of television are compromising the minds of everyone, causing people to slowly accept what they see as normal in the world's eyes. I can visualize God hanging his head in sadness over what Hollywood has done to the average TV viewer.

Fasting has removed me far from the desires I once had and has broken my carnal habits, like watching too much TV. He has delivered me from addictions from food; alcohol; over-the-counter drugs, like ibuprofen; and has taken my body and mind to a new and higher level of worship.

I know now more than ever before in my life how much desire I have within me to take care of the temple (my body) where the Holy Spirit resides for the purpose of giving God glory for who he made me to be. I am forever devoted in learning to not abuse my flesh and spirit with junk and harmful things. It is such a temporary, short-lived pleasure to eat or drink something that harms your body, but you do it because it tastes so good for the moment. Later down the road, you see results like weight gain, heart disease, cancer, diabetes, heartburn, premature aging, depression, lethargy, migraines, and more. Yes, nutrition affects all of those things more than genetics, but sometimes there are things that are inherited genetically.

My vow to you, Lord, is to take care of my temple more now than I have ever before, because you are my healer, my provider, my God, who will sustain me in my old age. Praise you, Father, my God in heaven, who is good. "And may he be to you a restorer of life and a nourisher of your old age" (Ruth 4:15, NKJV).

Day Twenty-Five

It's Friday morning, and I am moving slow and had another fire in the fireplace. The construction site across the street let me have scrap wood. That is a blessing for warm heat. I put my running shoes on and went for a run/walk because the Lord told me to start exercising to stimulate my soul, my body, and my mind. Fasting has kept me indoors praying, resting, and seeking him, and I needed exercise. It worked! Why would I ever doubt the Lord? He is so good.

My drive to The Dalles was good and safe but rainy. It was nice to see my daughter. I pray for her healing and restoration between her earthly father and her through my fasting while my prayers cried out to God the Father. I offer all that I am up to the Lord so he will answer my prayers. I ask for a restored unity for my family that only God can provide. "Restore us, O God; make your face shine upon us, that we may be saved" (Psalm 80:3, NIV).

There were challenges God had for me over the weekend while visiting family. I was dealing with several people who have no clue of the goodness of God. I endured foul language, worldly views, and immoral thinking. There was one young man who visited that weekend at my daughter's house who God is preparing for salvation because we talked a little bit about heaven, and he is scared of the end-times that he said someone told him about. He wants to go to heaven. I wanted to pray with him and share the plan of salvation, but there were many interruptions all around us. I do get to meet up with him again soon, so I pray I don't totally botch the window of opportunity and time God may have for me. I know God is going to cause great revival to spring forth within my daughter's house between her and her new husband that will extend and overflow to her friends! Praise be to God in heaven and our Lord, Jesus Christ. For he loves us so much.

After thoughts

> Death and life are in the power of the tongue, And those who love it will eat its fruit.
>
> Proverbs 18:21 (NASB)

A person's words, figuratively called the fruit of his mouth and the harvest from his lips, can benefit himself when his words are positive and uplifting. However, one's words (tongue) may bring death as well as life. A witness in a court, for example, can help determine by his words whether a defendant lives or dies. Those who love it (the tongue) refers to people who are talkative; they will suffer the consequences and eat the fruit of what they say. A man may do a great deal of good, or a great deal of hurt, both to others and to himself, according to the use he makes of his tongue. Many people cause their own death by a foul tongue, or the death of others by a false tongue; and, on the contrary, many of us have saved his or her own life, or procured the comfort of it, by a prudent gentle tongue, and saved the lives of others by a seasonable testimony or intercession for them. And, if by our words we must be justified or condemned, death and life are, no doubt, in the power of the tongue. Tongues were Aesop's best meat, and his worst. Men's words will be judged of by the affections in how they choose to speak; he that not only speaks aright (which a bad man may do to save his credit or please his company), but loves to speak so, speaks well of choice, and with delight, to him it will be life; and he that not only speaks amiss but loves to speak so (Ps. 52:4), to him it will be death. As we speak it we shall eat the fruit of it.

—*The Bible Knowledge Commentary:*
Old Testament
by John F. Walvoord and Roy B. Zuck

There are many references to the tongue in Proverbs. We should make an effort to read the chapters twelve and eighteen because they mention the tongue frequently, but you will want to follow the cross references and examine other verses as well. We so often take the wonderful gift of speech for granted and abuse an ability that ought to be guarded and used for the glory of God.

Before we consider some of the sins of the tongue, we ought to note the blessings of a godly tongue. This demands a godly heart, because the tongue only speaks what the heart treasures. When we make an effort to speak good things, the tongue is like valuable silver, a beautiful and fruitful tree of life, a refreshing well of water, and a healthy dose of medicine.

The tongue should be used for right purposes: bringing peace, giving wise reproof to those who hear, delivering lost souls from death, teaching people the things of the Lord, and carrying the good news of the gospel.

But Satan and the flesh want to control the tongue, and the results are sad. Perhaps more damage is done to lives, homes, and churches by the tongue than by any other means. It is sobering to realize that the tongue can be used to damage reputations and cause trouble when it ought to be used to praise God, pray, and witness to others about Christ. The tongue is a "little member" of the body (James 3:5), but it is one member that must be yielded to God as a tool of righteousness (Romans 6:12–13). Perhaps if we consider some of the sins of the tongue, it might encourage us to use our gift of speech more carefully.

We should all pray for an anointed tongue—one that speaks out encouragement and love for the edifying of those who listen to us.

As I began doing my study on this subject, it showed me many areas in my own life where I fall short—or better yet, I say to the Lord, I fall "long and hard on my face" before the glory of God in this area. Please, Lord, anoint my tongue to speak of the good things of you and of the life you gave me.

Luke 10:2 tells us that as we go out into the world, speaking and sharing the gospel, that Jesus will go with us, anointing and appointing us to speak his words and not ours. I pray for that anointing and speech that only comes from the Father!

I believe God has called me to a special ministry, and it cannot be carried out properly without his full blessing. Only God can open doors for me that no man can shut!

Let God anoint my tongue, and he will cause me to speak with divine authority, and never again will I say, "I am a weak and inadequate vessel." He shall put all the words into my mouth and my heart, and there will be no fear as the words leave my lips, because all the ears that hear will be filled to the full of God's message as it goes into their hearts.

I will only speak of the good in life that God will bring. Let my mouth speak encouragement and truth so that the ears of those listening will be blessed. Lord, always keep my tongue in check to remind me that it has the power to speak life or death.

Let truth be my way and love be in my actions. Anoint my mouth with your blessings, and send me out to the nations— making me your servant for the harvest. Use me and bless me so others may know you and follow you until the day of your return. Praise you, Jesus, for your words spoken here: "And He was saying to them, 'The harvest is plentiful, but the laborers are few; therefore beseech the Lord of the harvest to send out laborers in His harvest'" (Luke 10:2, NIV).

God wants us to speak the words of faith. He wants to put the words of knowledge and his wisdom on all our tongues. By speaking the words of our God from the Bible out loud, claiming your promises and your salvation to others who need to be saved will open doors that no man can shut. It is simple to speak, but be sure to speak what God puts in our mouth so that those who hear God's Word will let it enter them when otherwise they may have kept their hearts closed to the gospel's truth.

Once that door of another's heart is opened, you have the opportunity to plant the seed of faith, and it will birth a reborn heart and spring forth into eternal life.

My prayer for all who read this is:

> Lord, let my mouth learn to speak slower and put your thoughts to work before I utter words that have no purpose. Let my life and my speech reflect your love and your light. I want to express my changed life and changed heart by the way I live so that I can be a walking testimony of the power of the gospel. Teach me to labor for the gospel of Jesus Christ, and help me to speak truth, love, and wise words to those who are tender to your spirit and to those who also have hardened hearts who need to hear the word of truth that will pierce their hearts and let you come in and take charge of their life. Father, lead me to those you have chosen for the kingdom, those who are ready to hear about salvation. Praise you, Jesus. Amen

Day Twenty-Six

As of today, I have completed four weeks of fasting, and even though I am eating, I still am not without hunger, cravings, and extreme taste bud desires!

My diet consist of fruits, vegetables, salads, and whole grains. I am not eating any kind of bread, all dairy has been eliminated, and absolutely no meat or desserts of any kind.

My prayers have not changed, but the intensity has seemed to have decreased until tonight. It's been another divine reversal! I have prayed salvation for my family and for a major restoration to take place. My exact prayers kind of went like this: Lord, restore my family and bring me back to your original plan you had for me long ago, and I prayed many other restoring requests.

My thoughts were for my family, starting with my kids and their father, who has no real relationship with them. I remember even asking the Lord to turn my life inside out so he could use me, restore me as well, and my family, as it was in my youth.

At church today we had an altar call to come forward in prayer for those who are afflicted with loneliness. It felt like God's message was spoken just for me alone and He wanted to set me free in order for me to walk in perfect love and victory. So I went up and was prayed over. It was a root of abandonment that needed to be pulled up. I still have seeds of unworthiness that cause me to be unforgiving toward my parents. God has totally restored me, but it is up to me to give it to him at the altar and confess his power over that affliction, and then he will bring my family into the kingdom with me to his original plan.

Now I know why he gave me the scripture "the last shall be first." God is so good. I cried out so much pain tonight that I could feel it pressing out through the top of my skull. I put worship music on when I got home from church and praised God as he bathed me in his love and filled me with his spirit while he did the work in my heart and soul. All my dreams are coming to pass because I love him as I learn to obey him, and he loves me more than words could ever express. I have been redeemed all over again and renewed as a reminder of just how precious I am to the King.

His love is the only love that can fill you up.

I am so thankful that all day long, my cup overflows with the love of the Father, who keeps watch over my soul.

In this verse, God has given me insight: Out of five kids, I was the last one born from my mom. Even though I may be the last born, God has planned to make me the first to bring forth his plans for restoring the whole family (through fasting a fervent prayer) according to his plan and his good purpose. His purpose is unfolding and prophetically taking place in my life as I submit all my weaknesses to him to use me as I pray, seeking him for the family—for my whole family. God loves families. "So the last will be first, and the first last. For many are called, but few chosen" (Matthew 20:16, NKJV).

> But he said to me, "My grace is sufficient for you, for my power is made perfect in weakness." Therefore I will boast all the more gladly about my weaknesses, so that Christ's power may rest on me. That is why, for Christ's sake, I delight in weaknesses, in insults, in hardships, in persecutions, in difficulties. For when I am weak, then I am strong.
>
> 2 Corinthians 12:9–10 (NIV)

After thoughts

I began my fast after a life-changing conference at City Bible Church in Portland, Oregon. It was there that God touched my heart deep inside my soul. It felt as though he personally reached down and penetrated my chest through all my flesh and bones, and his fingers gently held my heart in his hand while he healed my thoughts, my motives, and my body. I don't think I have ever had the touch of God on me like I did on that day at any other time in my life before. It was in those most incredible four days that God called me out—out of the normal way of thinking and out of my carnal habits that hindered him from working in my life. He told me that the time had come for me to be serious about the salvation of this world and about my family's welfare for the kingdom. God's words to my heart said he was in a hurry. Not that God himself was in a hurry, but it translated to me later that day that he is coming soon and his coming will be like a flash, like the thief in the night and that he wants his beloveds to be ready and waiting.

He called me to seriousness—to a greater power he has given within me called prayer. He also said that prayers are powerful, especially when you pray the fervent prayer from your heart and soul. Fasting is a very powerful additive to prayer. It is total sacrifice to our Lord and shows him that we seek him first and foremost for all our needs and that we can do nothing without his help. Fasting is mentioned in the Bible one time for every three times prayer is mentioned. When you need things done supernaturally, I recommend getting serious with God and fasting and sending up your prayers like never before. It is grace alone that gave me strength for this. It taught me to put my self aside, shut my TV off, and pray every moment I am awake—even if it was in the car, shower, working, or wherever I was.

> So we fasted and sought our God concerning this matter, and He listened to our entreaty.
>
> Ezra 8:23 (NASB)

> So I gave my attention to the Lord God to seek Him by prayer and supplications, with fasting, sackcloth and ashes.
>
> Daniel 9:3 (NASB95)

Here are a few reasons why serious Christians should want to start fasting to the Lord. It is a calling, not a requirement since, yes, we are under grace, but Christ does call us to all things. Remember, he himself did not begin his ministry until after his forty-day fast in the wilderness. It released God's power in him through prayer and fasting. He was tempted by the devil several times, and he broke the bondage of the flesh and defeated the evil one before he went out to heal the sick, gave sight to the blind, and set people free!

First of all, the definition of fasting is a voluntary withdrawing from food and/or drink or other fleshly appetite for a specified period of time. But what is the reason for a fast in your life?

As we look at Scripture, in Exodus 34:27–28, we see clearly that Moses fasted on Mount Sinai in the wilderness as well for forty days before the Ten Commandments were given to him. When he came down from the mountain, it was clear that God had met with him because the skin on his face shone and the people were afraid to speak with him. When we stop to think about the glow and glory in Moses's face, it clearly speaks how much power was deposited in him by God after his fasting and prayer spent on holy ground with God.

> Then the Lord said to Moses, "Write down these words, for in accordance with these words I have made a covenant with you and with Israel. So he was there with the Lord forty days and forty nights; he did not eat bread or drink water. And

he wrote on the tablets the words of the covenant, the Ten Commandments.

> Exodus 34:27–28 (NASB)

Both Moses and Jesus began their earthly ministry with prayer and fasting, and they endured forty days.

Please note: I would never recommend forty days without food or water without medical and spiritual counsel.

> Then Jesus was led up by the spirit into the wilderness to be tempted by the devil. And when He had fasted forty days and forty nights, afterward He was hungry.
>
> Matthew 4:1–2 (NKJV)

> But the days will come when the bridegroom will be taken away from them; then they will fast in those days.
>
> Luke 5:35 (NKJV)

Though fasting is never commanded, Jesus assumed that the disciples would want to in order to see great things happen. But it's not something a Christian has to do but can choose to do, and I believe we need to be devoted and disciplined enough to want to fast. It is your total worship and sacrifice.

A normal fast is no food, only liquids like water and or diluted juice, etc.

> Then all the sons of Israel and all the people went up and came to Bethel and wept; thus they re-

mained there before the Lord and fasted that day until evening. And they offered burnt offerings and peace offerings before the Lord.

Judges 20:26 (NASB)

A one-day fast is a good place to start. One day fasting is usually water only for twenty-four hours.

Paul of Tarsus did a three-day fast right before he was saved and received back his sight. A partial fast is good if you have diabetes, hypoglycemia, or some other condition that precludes a normal fast. Some give up meats, breads, and dairy for a time. Eating only vegetables or just skipping a meal to spend time in prayer would be another example of a partial fast.

The absolute fast is what Moses went on for forty days. Nothing enters your mouth at all. This can be done *only* for a very short time; consult a doctor!

What is *your* purpose for fasting?

Your purpose should be to focus on God's will for your life as you present your request to him during extended times of prayer. Fasting without spending time in prayer is nothing more that going on a starvation or partial diet. You must pray.

Of course, there are physical benefits: Medical doctors are discovering more and more benefits to fasting because the body is designed to heal itself on a cellular level. As we eat and take in various toxins, processed foods, medicines, etc., we hold a certain amount of poisons in our cells, but when we fast, many of those things are flushed out of our systems. But if you want a spiritual benefit, make sure to take the time you would have spent eating and transfer it to prayer time.

> Jehoshaphat was afraid and turned his attention to seek the Lord, and proclaimed a fast throughout all Judah. So Judah gathered together to seek help from the Lord; they even came from all the cities of Judah to seek the Lord.
>
> 2 Chronicles 20:3–4 (NASB)

> When I heard these words, I sat down and wept and mourned for days; and I was fasting and praying before the God of heaven.
>
> Nehemiah 1:4 (NASB)

> Stop depriving one another, except by agreement for a time, so that you may devote yourselves to prayer, and come together again so that Satan will not tempt you because of your lack of self-control.
>
> 1 Corinthians 7:5 (NASB)

Another point made by this verse is that when we fast, it ought to be from *all* physical desires—not just food! Let go of the physical, and focus on the spiritual! Shut off your television during all your fasting! You will be shocked what you can accomplish in prayer and worship with *no* television distractions. Play worship music instead. Usually we fast and pray when we have a special need.

Day Twenty-Seven

The peace of God reigns in my life strongly today. It seems as if he has built a shield—a wall of protection—around me. I hunger constantly for the Lord's presence, for his daily provision and blessings to chase me down and overtake me. I can't get enough of him in my life. All my desires have turned to him. The desires of my heart are to know him and continue to bask my soul into the love God has for me. Lord, send your Holy Spirit to me and fill me up tonight. My prayer is for you, Lord, to fill me full with wisdom and strength so that I will know you better. Let me serve you through loving other people, people who need your love poured over them like running water. Praise you, Lord! Praise your name, and bless the God in heaven, who loves us unconditionally! Amen.

> Trust in the Lord with all your heart and lean not on your own understanding; in all your ways acknowledge him, and he will make your paths straight.
>
> Proverbs 3:5–6 (NIV)

Blessed is the man who finds wisdom, the man who gains understanding, for she is more profitable than silver and yields better returns than gold. She is more precious than rubies; nothing you desire can compare with her. Long life is in her right hand; in her left hand are riches and honor. Her ways are pleasant ways, and all her paths are peace. She is a tree of life to those who embrace her; those who lay hold of her will be blessed.

Proverbs 3:13–18 (NIV)

Day Twenty-Eight

I lay here in bed, and my body sighs. It is late, but the call of God is strong and keeps me awake to study, read the Word, and journal.

God is faithful when you call on him. He is so quick to show up when your desires for him are true and from the heart. You cannot fool God with empty words or try to hide anything from him. He sees everything you do in private, he knows your thoughts, and he hears your words and sees completely through your heart. It gives him glory when you lay it all out for him, and I mean *all*. We need to admit to God our faults (even though he already knows all of them), repent, and ask for forgiveness always. When we miss the mark or screw up things because of our own stupid ways and sin against the Holy Spirit, whom we grieve, then be quick to repent and lay it out there. God is eager and ready to forgive you. His mercies are new every morning! God already knows everything about us and what we are going to ask, but to hand it willingly to him makes him smile upon you, giving you favor. He knows that, with a willing heart, he has something to work with when you can humble yourself in all your faults, all your sins, and say to God, "That's ugly in my life. Please fix that for me because I need your help … I can't do it without you!" *And he will!*

All God wants is our hearts, our obedience, and for us to be willing to let him do the work in us. When I figured that out, I quit trying so hard to be "good" or be a super sister Christian, and I let God do all things through me and for me.

> Commit your way to the Lord; trust in him and he will do this: He will make your righteousness shine like the dawn, the justice of your cause like the noonday sun. Be still before the Lord and wait patiently for him; do not fret when men succeed in their ways, when they carry out their wicked schemes. Refrain from anger and turn from wrath; do not fret, it leads only to evil. For evil men will be cut off, but those who hope in the Lord will inherit the land.
>
> Psalm 37:5–9 (NIV)

Day Twenty-Nine

Focus, focus, focus!

God's plans for the future are good, for home and for well-being. I know this with all my heart. I pray for his plans to unfold and to fill my life with evidence of his awesome mercy and grace. God, give me strength to lean on you day after day. I ask you to continually hear my prayers for my family, my future, and to keep my heart new for you, Lord.

Use me for the kingdom, and teach me to be of service to others and not live a selfish and self-centered life that does nothing but consume. We are such a consumer society, and I want to instill in my heart and the hearts of others that it is relationships, love for other people, and Jesus Christ's salvation that matter in this life and the life to come.

Without that, life is meaningless! Without Christ, life is hopeless and downright scary. The world is frightening, if you depend on its ways to direct your path. Think about how crazy everything is right now with this world—the war on peace, the oil prices, food prices, all the disasters hitting various places on the earth. The hysteria of the world is doomed to stress out even more, especially with those people who don't know Christ.

In Christ, there is love, peace, joy, and the ability to endure long suffering—only from grace given by the Holy Spirit. Lord, teach me how to share the plan of salvation with people because so many need to turn to you to be saved before you return! And it is soon. Come to him today! Praise you, Lord. Amen.

> For I know the plans I have for you, says the Lord. They are plans for good and not for disaster, to give you a future and a hope. In those days when you pray, I will listen. If you look for me wholeheartedly, you will find me.
>
> Jeremiah 29:11–13 (NLT)

After thoughts

God's Main Purposes for Fasting

1. Fasting to get freedom from addictions.

Isaiah 58:6: "Loose the bands" (things you'd like to lay down but have been unable to).

"I've tried to quit smoking, but I can't!"

Try fasting!

Porn/alcohol/cussing throughout life.

Try fasting!

God has ordained that when we get serious about walking in victory, we demonstrate it through fasting, and then he knows we're serious!

2.   Fasting to solve problems.

"Undo heavy burdens" (also Isaiah 58:6).

Illnesses, messed-up finances, marriage in shambles, or a job solution?

When it seems hopeless and there's no way out, God will deal with all those in an instant—what you've stressed about for weeks and months or even years!

3.   Fasting for revival and soul winning.

Again Isaiah 58:6: "Let oppressed go free."

I challenge you to do this ... this week!

4.   Fasting to conquer mental and emotional problems.

Again, in Isaiah 58:6: "Break every yoke."

5.   Fasting to meet the physical needs of others.

Isaiah 58:7: "Deal," which means to share and to cut back once in a while and give that food or money to feed the poor.

6. Fasting for clearer insight in decision making.

This is different than problem solving. This is when you're seeking God's will in a major area of your life and you're at the fork in the road and don't know which way to go—job offers, transfers, dating, marriage, divorce, ministry, or what college to attend or if not to attend. Isaiah 58:8: "Light break forth." It's like God turns on the lights, and now you know what to do!

7. Fasting for health reasons or healing.

Have a loved one that's terminal? Family members plagued with constant health issues or your own health issues? Get serious and fast!

Fasting, for me, became my only resource to really draw near to the Lord and gain understanding and blessings over my family and me. I came from a family of dysfunction that I know now goes back several generations. Spiritual bondage over families will follow several generations, causing strongholds and yokes, choking out God's will.

I am praying and fasting for the Lord to release my family to the kingdom of God once and for all so that all bondages and yokes be broken off, the captives will be set free, all our health will spring forth, and for God's provision to be in abundance.

I believe in salvation for the whole family and for my children's children. That is a huge request that takes serious endeavors and serious prayer, devotion, and worship of our Creator. Serious faith. Serious expectation.

Let the light break forth. Do not be afraid of what fasting may feel like. It becomes a true form of worship. There were days that had passed that all I could do was sit in a chair and wait on God to show up because I was too weak to pray, to think, or do anything but sit there. God will honor your time no matter what you do because fasting is a constant prayer offered up. During the time I usually spent eating, I would go to prayer instead. When I would normally turn on the TV, I went into prayer instead. It became powerful.

The Lord Almighty, holy Creator, who knows all of our needs, will provide them to those who seek him with the fervent heart. He will show up and be the God that we all read about in the Word. His Word is true, and his promises are real promises!

Seek him and you will find him!

Day Thirty

I woke up feeling all alone, even though I know in my heart that God is always with me. His plan is ready to unfold in my life. Here I am, Lord. Use me. Make me your servant, your vessel for the kingdom.

I am living on pure faith and hope in all things, knowing my prayers are at the foot of him who loves me. His love will never leave me, his love is everlasting, and I know it is his love that takes me to my knees and fills my heart with joy, and my eyes fill up with tears. I bask in worship, and his presence cleanses every thought, every hurt, and all my sin and makes me new. His mercies are new every morning!

> Through the Lord's mercies we are not consumed, because His compassions fail not. They are new every morning; great is your faithfulness. The Lord is my portion, says my soul, therefore I hope in Him!
> Lamentations 3:22–24

I long to stay in the moment of worship always, forever, every minute, but I know I must face the reality of human living in a body of flesh on this planet, facing daily ups and downs and pressing on for the things of God until he comes back. Perhaps I am one who is focused on the things of the kingdom so much that it has penetrated my mind to the point where people think I am crazy or out there. I am happy to rejoice in being overzealous or crazy in love with the Lord. He is my rock, and he loves me like no other. He is my strength and my focus every waking minute of every day. When you are in love with another person, you feel the butterflies and the joy inside your heart because you have the love and affection of another person who has captured your heart. That is what I am feeling for the love that Jesus has provided me. Until we get that in our heads, we will never really understand the love of Jesus. *His* love is abounding, real, and everlasting. He loves us so much—more than any possible love you could ever imagine is in *him*.

> But now, thus says the Lord, who created you, O Jacob, and He who formed you, O Israel: Fear not, I have redeemed you; have called you by your name; You are Mine.
>
> Isaiah 43:1 (NKJV)

> And you have not seen Him, you love Him, and though you do not see Him now, but believe in Him, you greatly rejoice with joy inexpressible and of glory,
>
> 1 Peter 1:8 (NASB)

As I ponder and think on why I sometimes feel alone, perhaps it is my past trying to creep back into my soul, my mind, and thoughts. Being a girl that was abandoned by both parents at different times and at different levels makes me vulnerable to the attacks of Satan to remind me of such things. But grace and love have abounded in my life from the mercy God shows those who love him. I don't care about what happened to me anymore because Jesus has changed me. It is good that God has healed the wounds. There is a song I love that sings, "Heal the wounds, but leave the scars," as a reminder of how great his mercies are. But I refuse to look back at my wounds in a mournful manner, in a way that takes you there negatively. All that has happened is for the glory of God and to speak of the good things he does and how he redeems those who come to him. He promised me that my mess shall become my message to all who are afflicted with the pain of abandonment and loneliness. God is awesome. "But Jesus said to him, No one, after putting his hand to the plow and looking back, is fit for the kingdom of God" (Luke 9:62, NASB).

With every disappointment I have seen, there will be treasure. The enemy slips in the cracks of our life to constantly say to us, "All is lost." I say, "No," to the enemy, because *much* will be gained by saying, "*Yes*," to God's Word because he doesn't lie and he is *faithful*.

I refuse the temptation to brood over what I have lost and what is now gone in my life. It has been turned over to the Lord and passed into the area of *his* sovereignty. Today's a new day, and all the challenges coming our way will require undivided attention.

Give no time or thoughts to darkness and depression of what you lost because it will undermine your well-balanced growth and mental strength of your soul. We have nothing to be disappointed in because we have the hope of his coming in glory to take us home. Our crown awaits us in the kingdom to come. Continue to always look up.

My prayer today:

Lord, your grace always comes when I need it most. I will no longer look back, as did Lot's wife, who turned to a pillar of salt. Satan wants us to look back and wallow in our past mistakes so he can take our future joy. Our future is with you, Lord, our faith, our hope, love, peace, joy, and the kingdom promised to us. I will press forward to hear your voice and do what I can today. I will not regret my past but rejoice in *your* hand on me for my future. The darkroom of my life has been filled with *your* light, and now I see where you are taking me.

Praise you, Lord.

After thoughts

> Seek the Lord while He may be found; Call upon Him while He is near.
>
> Isaiah 55:6 (NASB)

I had a desperate need for knowing God. He calls us, and he woos us into his presence, but we must have our ears open and our hearts softened. We need ears that hear so that we do not miss the window of opportunity of his calling and presence while he may be found. We find him when we hear him, and when you hear him, you will respond to his voice, his word, and his touch on your life.

I believe there is a window of opportunity when he calls us. If we ignore him, he will move on to the next available heart that longs for his presence. When he knocks and we do not answer, he moves on to the next available heart that longs to hear from him.

God is so good to stand before us when we open the door for him to come into our life. Seek him in fervent and frequent prayer. Praying lifts the soul and feeds the spirit, and it gives God glory. It sends our voice to heaven to activate the commands of the holy angels to do our bidding! It is our voice to the King on high, who will grant us our request when we go to him and believe he hears us. Therefore, let us draw near with confidence to the throne of grace so that we may receive mercy and find grace to help in time of need (Hebrews 4:16, NASB 95).

So many times we feel like we cannot go to God in prayer because of guilt or condemnation. We are washed white as snow under the blood of Jesus! So when you pray, pray a bold prayer! Pray to the one who loves you and wants to hear you talk with him. We are blessed with the privilege to go to the throne of grace boldly and ask God for what it is we need and want. He knows our request and our needs before we even utter one word, so why not step out boldly to him and say, "Here I am, Lord," and ask and pray with confidence. Pray without ceasing (1 Thessalonians 5:17, NASB).

I always thought that this meant to be on your knees, praying constantly! Wow, that would be impossible. I believe God wants us to be in a state of mind that involves him constantly in everyday situations every moment we walk, talk, and breathe.

What does praying without ceasing look like? It is a constant conscious mindset that God is with you. When you are doing your daily routine, it should involve your thoughts with God. Simple things like, "Help me, Lord, to find a good parking spot among all this traffic," "Lord, please go with me today as I work and do my job. Let people see me as a light in a dark world," "Lord, watch my steps today and keep my mouth from saying wrong things," and "Lord, keep me from getting angry at the grocery checker for being so slow." In everything we do, it should include God. He wants to be involved in every thought. He wants us to ask him questions about every area of our life. Pray without ceasing! It is easy when he lives inside you. Jesus is a voice in our hearts that should be our first love, and we need to talk to him all day long.

Prayer is your constant awareness and daily request as the day goes about as business as usual. It is our ultimate form of worship to be in his presence on a minute-to-minute life. God is so good! He wants to hear from you.

Day Thirty-One

There are only ten days left for me, and it seems like my time in the Lord has gone by fast—actually faster than one even realizes. It has passed so quickly, like one day. I don't want the blessings and anointed presence of God to ever leave me! My body has experienced some changes throughout the past month. Some good; some not so good. Eating again after twenty days of no food was a shock, and now I have been eating for ten days and still am going slow and careful as to what enters my mouth.

I offer up to you, Lord, all that I am today, tomorrow, and forever. Your path has been laid out before me. Give me wisdom to walk on it and never wander off your plan for my life. Create in me a clean heart, like King David cried out to you. Cleanse my thoughts, and forgive me, Lord, for all my sins now and the ones you know I will commit in the future. Please keep me from sin and evil in my life, because my desire is to follow you, obey, and always hear your voice speaking over my life.

When I am weary, you lift me up, and when my body aches, you fill it up with your presence and miraculous renewing strength.

I will praise you all day long, even when I do not feel like it, because you are my God, my everlasting strength, my place of protection, and my shelter of love when no one else is loving me. Your love is a forever-lasting love.

You made me what I am, and you love me as I am. You know everything about me, as well as all my thoughts—even though they might be good or bad. You love me so much that it is hard to comprehend at times.

Praise you, Father, because you have taken all my sins from me through the precious blood of our Lord, Jesus. I offer my life to obey you and be with you for all eternity.

Restore and renew your vows!

> The one who has My commands and keeps them is the one who loves Me. And the one who loves Me will be loved by My Father. I also will love him and will reveal Myself to him.
>
> John 14:21 (HCSB)

There seems to be days when I wait on the Lord and think, *Where are you, Lord? I don't hear you.* All I hear is the wind in the trees or the babbling brook.

God spoke to me, and said, "I am never silent. I am always near. You are deaf! I am always speaking. You are sometimes not attuned to listen to me when you should."

"Oh my Lord. Forgive me!" I said.

I sit alone and feel sorry for myself in all my loneliness at times, grieving my solitude. But he has not left me—never. It is my own flesh that has become insensitive or tuned out to the voice of my *Lord*.

Praise you for your love, Lord. Forgive me for my selfish attitude thinking you are only near on certain days when in fact you are near every minute. Teach me, Lord, to not be insensitive to your voice. Let me always know you are near and that your divine plan has a time and a purpose to unfold for my life in your timing. Please keep me under your care and watch over my life, give me wisdom, and help me to discern what is right and wrong for my life.

In Jesus's precious name. Amen.

After thoughts

> Jesus said to him, "If you wish to be complete, go and sell your possessions and give to the poor, and you will have treasure in heaven; and come, follow Me."
>
> Matthew 19:21 (NASB)

In Christ, we are complete and have all we need. So many times we lean on what the world has for us, and it feels real, and it is visible. The things of the world are visual, touchable, and temporarily comforting, but in the spirit world, we need none of what the world has to offer, because when we die, we don't take any of it with us. We take our soul that never dies.

God knows we need things like food, shelter, and clothing. But when you put it all aside and lean on him completely and fully, it all fades and his purpose and his provision become more vivid and important. Keep in mind that by withholding your gifts and offerings to God, you are robbing him and the whole kingdom.

> I the Lord do not change. So you, O descendants of Jacob, are not destroyed. Ever since the time of your forefathers you have turned away from my decrees and have not kept them. Return to me, and I will return to you, says the Lord Almighty. But you ask, How are we to return? Will a man rob God? Yet you rob me. But you ask, How do we rob you? In tithes and offerings. You are under a curse—the whole nation of you—because you are robbing me. Bring the whole tithe into the storehouse, that there may be food in my house. Test me in this, says the Lord Almighty, and see if I will not throw open the floodgates of heaven and pour out so much blessing that you will not have room enough for it. I will prevent pests from devouring your crops, and the vines in your fields will not cast their fruit, says the Lord Almighty. Then all the nations will call you blessed, for yours will be a delightful land, says the Lord Almighty.
>
> Malachi 3:6–12 (NIV)

During my fast, as I prayed and sought after God's complete presence, I found the things of the world fading and becoming smaller, becoming less important.

Eternity is reality; it is what we need to focus on. Giving of your time to others in need is an eternal act—it is love. Giving your worldly possessions away is an eternal act of love. And giving away your money is a sign that you are not hanging on to the things of this world. God owns all we have; he is the one who gives us all things. We breathe his air! We need to give back to him what he so freely has given us. Tithe your money to him, and give your gifts and time to his kingdom, and he will make you rich in all areas of your life, including wisdom, health, finances, and peace in your soul.

We are so blessed in America! So many people do not know what it feels like to be in need or know what hunger pain is. While on that long journey with God, I felt hunger pain so deep inside my physical body that it showed me how giving is one of the most important acts of obedience that we can submit to God. He commands us to love and to give. He also promises us that if we give, he will fill our barns and vats to the overflow of abundance and provide all we need in life. His promises are true.

> Now this I say, he who sows sparingly will also reap sparingly, and he who sows bountifully will also reap bountifully. Each one must do just as he has purposed in his heart, not grudgingly or under compulsion, for God loves a cheerful giver.
> 2 Corinthians 9:6–7 (NASB)

> But whoever has the world's goods, and sees his brother in need and closes his heart against him, how does the love of God abide in him?
> 1 John 3:17 (NASB)

Day Thirty-Two

Oh precious love of the Father, who has kept me strong among the evil one. As he prowls around, I pray protection over my loved ones and all my family. You are holy, and you are faithful, Lord. I will remain strong, as I dedicate my life and my eating habits, and all my life will represent your love for me.

You bought me at a price, and my mind, soul, and body belong to you as I worship you through the sacrifice of my living body. My body is the temple of the Holy Spirit and a place where you dwell—a place where I can commune with you, Jesus.

I want to always remember to sacrifice the pleasures of my mouth by not polluting the body with the unnecessary things of this world but to feed it healthy living food. It is equally important to feed my body as well as I feed my soul with God's Word.

I love you, Lord, and I know now that all I have belongs to you. All my strength comes from you, and I want to fill my life, my mind, and my soul with all of your goodness.

In Jesus Christ's holy name. Amen.

Day Thirty-Three

June 14th, 2008. Today is my daughter's wedding day. A beautiful day it will be.

I sit in the morning sun and marvel at all of God's creation. I am marveling the beauty here on eighty acres of quiet solitude, with nature and spectacular views of the mountains, with majestic Mt. Hood shining in the morning sunlight as my backdrop.

The warmth of the sun and sounds all around me are evidence of God's world he created. The hummingbirds are in such large numbers that they sound like a huge beehive buzzing all around me, fighting for their individual times to feed from the feeder.

All the birds sing with their different chatters and songs and joyful tunes. The squirrels fight for food under the birdfeeders by the trees as they frolic and play, not having a care in this world.

The sky is painted deep blue, with no clouds in sight, as the snow-capped Mt. Hood towers over the valley.

God sits in heaven, looking down on all his creation, and I know he made all of this for us to enjoy and marvel over. His wonderful hands paint the color of the flowers and dress the fields with green grass as the deer walk through, eating in the cool morning air.

With all this beauty and all the detail of its wonder, I know that no one has any excuse and no reason to say that we do not have a Creator and a God in heaven. For all creation has a Creator and Master who planned all of this, who spoke and it came to be. The beauty on earth, the colors of the rainbow, the stars, and galaxies are all his! We are his, and we shall live as each day belongs to him.

Day Thirty-Four

Oh my sweet Jesus in heaven, I pray to you today for mercy for all my prayers that go up to heaven. Please hear me as I seek your face.

All weekend, I stayed away from the rich foods at my daughter's wedding. I feel healthy from God's grace and his provision of strength he has given me through all these days of fasting.

I am really finding strength to eat wholesome, living food as God continues to heal my health and my soul. I will never again sacrifice or neglect my time spent with him, who truly loves me more than I could ever think or imagine, because it was his life he gave up for me so that I might live and live with freedom and joy.

I am tired from all the traveling, and as I lie here alone in my bed, I realize each day that I am above ground is another day God has allowed me to enjoy. I will enjoy every day he gives me and never waste my days being depressed, angry, or sad, because I could be gone tomorrow. Then if I die, what good is it to waste my energy on futile things while on earth? God wants me to be joyful. The joy of the Lord is my strength.

Jesus commands us to love. It will change your life, if you truly learn to let go and live filled with his love.

Teach me, Lord, to not waste energy on things that have no importance, empty talk, or worry about the approval of others. I strive for your approval only and want to do your will, Lord, and not serve people as a people pleaser but a true and faithful God pleaser.

Give me strength to press on each day, as I sometimes feel so alone in an earthly sense. It is *your* love and presence that sustains me each day, Father. Your love and grace are sufficient for me until you come back for us.

Day Thirty-Five

My Father is glorified by this, that you bear much
fruit, and so prove to be My disciples.

John 15:8 (NASB95)

For every door God opens for me, I will enter and go
through. His spirit will speak through me, and I will open
my mouth that gives all the glory to you, Lord God, as
you guide the words that roll off my lips.

Now that you have watered me and I have grown in
your ways, I know you expect me to bear much fruit and
produce beautiful flowers. My fruit will bear beauty and
will be the signs and wonders of your spirit, Lord. You
will be manifested in my life, as it proves as a symbol that
the spirit truly rules in my heart. It is the true fulfillment
and your original plan for my life. You give me restoration, and it is my destiny to follow you. I was designed by
my Creator to do his good works. Anything less would be
failure and disappointment to my King.

To just live my life for myself alone is not enough; it does not satisfy. For I was created to excel and expand the gifts given to me by God in order that it passes on blessings to those around me and expands the kingdom to come.

My prayer today, Lord, is for more direction. My most important worship is to follow you day by day, and when that gets hard, I will take it hour by hour.

Father, open those doors that are divine and of your spirit so that I may pass through them.

Praise you, Father! In Jesus's name. Amen!

Day Thirty-Six

God is always watching. His hand guides and steers us down his path. Listen closely to his quiet, still voice, and he will direct you in the way he wants you to go.

> Make me know Your ways, O Lord; Teach me Your paths. Lead me in Your truth and teach me, For You are the God of my salvation; For You I wait all the day. Remember, O Lord, Your compassion and Your lovingkindnesses, For they have been from of old. Do not remember the sins of my youth or my transgressions; according to Your lovingkindness remember me, for Your goodness' sake, O Lord.
>
> Psalm 25:4–7 (NASB)

Day Thirty-Seven

Every day is a challenge to hear God's voice living in this fast-paced, carnal, and cold society. His strength is what keeps the light shining bright within me.

> Do all things without grumbling or disputing; so that you will prove yourselves to be blameless and innocent, children of God above reproach in the midst of a crooked and perverse generation, among whom you appear as lights in the world,
>
> Philippians 2:14–15 (NASB)

Day Thirty-Eight

I love you, Lord, and I want to spend my days worshiping you and giving you praise for my life. Your blessings are all around me, and I will make my mouth speak of the good things of God.

> My soul exalts the Lord, and my spirit has rejoice in God my Savior. For He has had regard for the humble state of His bondslave; For behold, from this time on all generations will count me blessed. For the Mighty One has done great things for me; And holy is His name. And His mercy is upon generation after generation toward those who fear Him. He has done mighty deeds with His arm; He has scattered those who were proud in the thoughts of their heart. . He has brought down rulers from their thrones, and has exalted those who were humble. He has filled the hungry with good things; and sent away the rich empty-handed.
>
> Luke 1:46–53 (NASB)

Praise God, everybody! Applaud God, all people! His love has taken over our lives; God's faithful ways are eternal. Hallelujah!

Psalm 117:1–2 (The Message)

Praise the Lord, all nations! Glorify Him, all peoples! For great is His faithful love to us; the Lord's faithfulness endures forever.

Hallelujah!

Psalm 117:1–2 (HCSB)

Day Thirty-Nine

Father, I pray that my mouth be tamed and bridled so that it speaks truth, love, and not harm to anyone.

Let my mind and ears hear and my mouth be slow to speak so that I will listen more.

I want to hear your voice, whether it be that sweet whisper you breathe into me that provides life to my bones and nourishment to my spirit or the sounding thunder that shakes the heavens when you speak. Let your voice be heard.

I pray your power to take hold of my life as I speak your decree into and over my life. Let your will be done to me according to your Word.

Let your power and your righteousness reign in my life, and bless the lives that I come in contact with. Pour your blessings out, and keep your precepts and your loving ways on my heart.

Break the chains of the religious spirit over our nation and over our people, Lord, and release the freedom over our worship and the freedom you gave us through your death on the cross. *Freedom.*

Praise you, Lord!

The Spirit of the Lord God is upon me, Because the Lord has anointed me To bring good news to the afflicted; He has sent me to bind up the brokenhearted, To proclaim liberty to captives And freedom to prisoners; To proclaim the favorable year of the Lord And the day of vengeance of our God; to comfort all who mourn

Isaiah 61:1–2 (NASB)

It was for freedom that Christ set us free; therefore keep standing firm and do not be subject again to a yoke of slavery.

Galatians 5:1 (NASB)

And you will know the truth, and the truth will make you free.

John 8:32 (NASB)

So if the Son makes you free, you will be free indeed.

John 8:36 (NASB)

O Lord, surely I am Your servant, I am Your servant, the son of Your handmaid, You have loosed my bonds.

Psalm 116:16 (NASB)

And I will walk at liberty, For I seek Your precepts.

Psalm 119:45 (NASB)

Forty Days of Praise

Lord, I made it forty days under nothing but your grace! Your grace was on me. I am now waiting on you, Lord, to fulfill my prayers now. I wait in high expectation. Some have already manifested, and some prayers are in action.

Everything else I know is at the altar, laying before your feet in heaven, being delivered to you by the holy angels who do your work.

I ask for a refreshing and a renewal and restored strength to come over me. I am weary, but your joy fills my soul, because my days with you have been really wonderful. I would not turn the clock back, nor do I regret the pain and struggle the fast put me through.

You gave me grace.

My days fasting are forever with you, as my living sacrifice was offered up in total submission with a sincere heart. I long to see what is to come next while I live on earth. Your power has broken all chains and strongholds over my life and has filled me with victory and a deeper love that gave me understanding. It brought my spirit close to you, and I felt your presence so strong at moments that all I could do was cry. Thank you, Father! Praise you!

Jesus, I love you for your sacrifice on the cross for me. Your life gave me life for all eternity. Yours is the one and only holy sacrifice I will ever focus on. You are my Savior, my refuge, and you gave me hope, and I know you are with me always. Come soon for us, Lord Jesus. "And behold, I am coming quickly. Blessed is he who heeds the words of the prophecy of this book" (Revelation 22:7, NASB).

Amen!

June 21, 2008

After thoughts

As I closed in my words for this journey, I realized how fast and how miraculous it was that God gave me words to share and how it all flowed like a fresh stream from him.

In every situation I endured or will endure in the future, I learned it is my duty and my God-given responsibility to confront it and face it with grace and dedication to him who strengthens me to turn every experience into a spiritual victory that gives Jesus Christ all the glory!

You are not powerless, and you are not in a box, but in the world to do his will and not your own. I am the King's daughter, and it is my prerogative to strengthen my mind, renew my life through the Word, and to carry out his assignments.

The evil in this world has no power over me because the Word of God speaks power over my life, which needs to come out of my mouth with faith and with power. The attitude you decide to take on for each day will determine the outcome, so take on the whole armor of God, and believe he can make all things possible in your life. You must speak and think as the Word of God speaks and thinks! "For nothing will be impossible with God" (Luke 1:37, NASB).

> For nothing will be impossible with God.
>
> Luke 1:37 (NASB)

> You are from God, little children, and you have conquered them, because the One who is in you is greater than the one who is in the world.
>
> 1 John 4:4 (HCSB)

You were bought at a price through the blood of Jesus Christ, and I pray that you will be sprinkled with his grace and power. Our life is not our own, but we belong to the Most High in heaven. I pray that the Word of God will bring you constant guidance when you are in doubt. So you must remember that *he* chose you, and if *he* chose you, believe you are blessed. And Mary said, "'Behold, the bond-slave of the Lord; may it be done to me according to your word.' And the angel departed from her" (Luke 1:38, NASB).

We should never run from God because of our failure to do his will. His mercies are new every morning. If you are reading this and are not a child of Jesus Christ, repent now, because there is still time. If you are a Christian and not following the will of God, repent and come back! Yes, he will take you in. I had turned my back on God for over twenty-six years and almost kept my heart far from him because I was ashamed of my failure and my sins. Do not abandon your heart's desire for righteousness because of your failures. Don't claim that your sins are not forgivable, because they are. The blood of Jesus is the most powerful act of love God gave you—it's a free gift. God sees you as white as snow, as pure and holy children under the blood of Jesus seated at the right hand of him in heaven. God gives us grace and his Holy Spirit to lift us above our despair. He gives you a song of praise in your heart and a hope for the future. All you need to do is repent, ask for his forgiveness, and fall before the living God, who will hear you and come to you, if you ask him. Praise him forever.

> To proclaim the year of the Lord's favor and the day of vengeance of our God, to comfort all who mourn, and provide for those who grieve in Zion—to bestow on them a crown of beauty instead of ashes, the oil of gladness instead of mourning, and a garment of praise instead of a spirit of despair. They will be called oaks of righteousness, and planting of the Lord for the display of his splendor.
> Isaiah 61:2–3 (NIV)

> Though the mountains move and hills shake, My love will not be removed from you and My covenant of peace will not be shaken, says your compassionate Lord.
> Isaiah 54:10 (HCSB)

> For sin shall not be master over you, for you are not under law but under grace.
> Romans 6:14 (NASB)

Afterword

Before I began this fasting journey, I had no idea that I would ever write a book. My words ran onto the pages like water flowing from a stream. God's Word penetrated me, and His presence led me here today. Now I look back at the special time that was reserved for my Savior. Yes, that is what fasting is. It's reservations you make with the King. It's your appointment to fulfill an expectation. It is a time of true worship. If you can give that to God, you will experience His presence like no other time you spend with Him or for Him. I love going to church to worship and hear the Word, but fasting, praying and giving to God is a refreshing emprise. It heals the soul, it answers prayers, it cleans the body and the mind and wakes up the spirit within you. It opens windows in heaven you have never seen through before. It is an unsupervised supernatural enterprise that will take you beyond what your mind can capsulate. Fasting becomes an exaggerated and supplemented euphoric experience that happens when you give God the power to show up during desperate times.

Before I gave my life up for Christ, I used to regret my past and wish that I could turn the clock back or rewrite my history book. I used to fantasize that I could erase each one of my mistakes because I did not like who I was or what I went through. I felt guilt and shame for all I did and for the things I did not do. But I still could not change the past, only my future. I would pray to God to please take away the shame and try to hide who I really was. I didn't want anyone to know the real me and see the ugliness that I hid inside my mind. Now it's all just a memory of where God has brought me from. The things He has brought me out of are now a testimony of His grace and His mercy that extends to anyone who calls out to him. It keeps me on my knees to just know where I came from and where He is taking me. Even though I live in freedom, I want my past to remind me of His goodness and His greatness. God is so good. He heals the wounds no matter how deep and how painful our scars have been imbedded into us. It's all just a reminder of how merciful His healing grace is. And just when you think you have been healed, God goes even deeper. His love for us never ends and His care over us is ongoing. It's what makes us be fruitful.

I have not lived a life that deserves honor and merits, nor can I boast about anything I have accomplished. It has all been stepping stones from God. My life was a pile of rubble before I gave it to the Lord. I don't take pride in myself, but only in His Glory for the favor He has shone down on me. I pray that I will never forget what He has done for me, even though there was pain and suffering. He used all my mistakes and all my self-destructive patterns that hurt me and turned them into the good things He has for my future. There is joy and beauty in my life now because of Christ Jesus. I was broken and torn apart until I called out to the one redeemer who heals our wounds. God has ignited a fire in my spirit, and my prayer is to make a world of difference to those in my life and through my life. I pray He begins with me and that my heart will be changed every day. The opposite of change is stagnation. So, God, begin with me, please. Wash me and lead me. Keep my heart in the light and never let deception be a part of my life. As my walk with you grows, may I continue to fast and pray to be an encourager for everyone and be excellent for you Lord, because you deserve excellence.

The Lord is all we need in this life because it is He who will be with us in the next life. It is vital that we live a life of faith and believe God and not the world. It is our faith that pleases God. Our faith keeps us in alignment with God and gives us hope. Our hope creates a desire to have more of the things of God. Love is the relevant evidence that you are living in peace with yourself and God. Loving others is produced through faith and believing that God will bless you abundantly. Love covers over many sins, and it is the very essence of God's persona.

Loved ones in Christ, you will never walk alone when you let Jesus take your hand. As I have gone through this journey and the walk with Him through fasting and prayer, I have learned to trust Him finally. Trust creates a calm spirit and forces anxiety to leave. Stress is no longer my ruler or my demon. God will show up when you trust him fully in all things. Fasting and Praying will change your perspective and interpretation of what it means to walk closely with Christ.

We all fall short and sometimes relapse in this life, but Jesus is right there to pick you up. Cling to him with your life. His mercies are new every morning. You will never walk alone. Take the risk and trust Him with your desires. He longs to give you the hopes and desires of your dreams because He is the one who put them in you. Embrace the joy of your salvation and cry out in gladness that salvation is here today for you. It is here like heaven on earth and on earth like it is in heaven. We must believe these things in order to grow. It is faith, hope, and love.

The dark days are gone and I no longer visit the darkroom of my life. God is light, and in Him all things are made known. There is no more confusion, and the curtain is taken away from our eyes. I see His love like no other love in this world. His strength carries me to the next level. God's goodness is endless, and He will extend a hand to help you, heal you, and fill your soul with joy. Wrapping your mind around the mind of God will shield you with His armor and His strength in all you do.

The Bible is God's love letter, so read it daily. Let it resonate and seep into your life like a sponge taking up water. Let God's forgiveness dissolve your sin like melting snow. Know in your heart that He loves you deeply and forever. There is nothing you can ever do that will cause God to not love you. When you realize how much He really loves you, then you will experience an intimacy of peace with Him. The heavens will open up and pour out such blessing upon you that you will see, feel, and know that all things are possible to those who believe. Here are my words of prayer for you. May your prayer and fasting life be enlarged, amplified, and strengthened as you embark on your own journey with Father God, Jesus Christ, and the Holy Spirit.

Jesus is faithful. Praise you, Lord.

You were faithful to me all the years I had my back turned on you. My failures and my sins weighed so heavy on me that I feared rejection if I was to turn back to you. You healed me, you comforted me, and you reassured me that you would never forsake me as all have done throughout my whole life.

You did all that for me, as well as shedding your blood for me on the cross, all before I gave one day for you. Your love was given to me first before I loved you. You saved me when I almost gave up my life. You redeemed me when I felt hopeless. My despair has miraculously and truthfully been lifted by you Lord.

Thank you. Praise you, Jesus, for your kingdom that is to come. Your will be done on this earth, as it is in heaven.

Please never doubt in the existence and power of God. Heaven and hell are real, and God is speaking to those whose hearts are open to be transformed.

When you shut the cover of this book, may the God of our Lord, Jesus Christ, shine on your life and bless you, and may His Holy Spirit speak to you and lead you into life eternal!

In Jesus's name I pray. *Amen*!

When they saw him, they worshiped him, but some of them doubted! Jesus came and told his disciples, "I have been given all authority in heaven and on earth. Therefore, go and make disciples of all the nations, baptizing them in the name of the Father and the Son and the Holy Spirit. Teach these new disciples to obey all the commands I have given you. And be sure of this: I am with you always, even to the end of the age."

Matthew 28:17–20 (NLT)

He who testifies to these things says, "Yes, I am coming quickly." Amen.

Come, Lord Jesus. The grace of the Lord Jesus be with all. Amen.

Revelation 22:20–21 (NASB)

Begin Your Journey

As you seek the Lord and journey on your own three-day, seven-day, twenty-one-day, or forty-day fast, remember to keep a daily journal and record each day as the Lord speaks to you.

Before you begin, examine your heart, and ask yourself, "Why am I fasting?

Am I fasting because God is leading me? Are there things in my life that need to be given over to God? Am I in crisis?"

Whatever your calling is for your fast, remember to write down the top three things you are laying on the altar and give them up totally to God. He is able to change your situations, your life, your habits, and answer your prayers, but when you fast and pray, it will take you into a closeness with the heavenly Father that brings joy, peace, and spiritual nourishment like nothing you have ever felt before. Your fasting and praying time is offered up to God for all eternity, because it is the greatest sacrifice when you become serious in getting God to hear you. He will pour his grace upon you in a way that is supernatural, and then your journey with him is taken to a new level of his light!

Please check with your doctor or health professional before beginning a long, extended fast.

May God bless you and keep you in his arms while you seek his presence and voice.

Love in Christ Jesus,

Kelly

Seek the Lord while he may be found;
Call on Him while he is near.

Isaiah 55:6 (NIV)

What area of your life is holding you back from serving God with all your heart and all your soul and all your mind?

_____

_____

_____

_____

_____

_____

_____

_____

_____

_____

_____

_____

_____

_____

_____

For if you forgive men when they sin against you,
your heavenly Father will also forgive you.

Matthew 6:14 (NIV)

Is there anyone in your life you need to forgive today? Ask God to reveal any hidden hurts that keep you hostage in your heart and for his love to fill up that place of brokenness. Forgiving others for offending you will bring healing to your body as well.

_____

_____

_____

_____

_____

_____

_____

_____

_____

_____

_____

_____

> This kind does not go out except by prayer and fasting.
>
> Matthew 17:21 (NKJV)

Is God calling out for you to remove obstacles, habits, or idols that hinder your walk with him? Let God's instructions have precedence over comfort. Consider to seek him today through prayer and fasting.

_____

_____

_____

_____

_____

_____

_____

_____

_____

_____

_____

_____

_____

_____

For whoever desires to save his life will lose it, but whoever loses his life for My sake and the gospel's will save it.

Mark 8:35 (NKJV)

Are you really serving the living God? Do you have one foot in the world and one foot in the church? What areas would you want to change if Jesus was sitting with you now?

_____

_____

_____

_____

_____

_____

_____

_____

_____

_____

_____

_____

_____

_____

_____

> What things so ever ye desire, when ye pray, believe that ye receive them, and ye shall have them.
> Mark 11:24 (KJV)

Sometimes we do not totally and completely trust God to supply our every need. Do you have a childlike faith in the Creator, or do you live with doubt?

_____

_____

_____

_____

_____

_____

_____

_____

_____

_____

_____

_____

_____

_____

_____

To shine on those living in darkness and in the shadow of death, to guide our feet into the path of peace.

Luke 1:79 (NIV)

We live in a world that is full anxiety, stress, and immoral pressures that seem to surround us like an evil army. How does it make you feel for your future, and is there any area in your life that you need Jesus to give you peace? Pray for his peace that surpasses all understanding.

_____

_____

_____

_____

_____

_____

_____

_____

_____

_____

_____

Launch out into the deep and let down your nets
for a catch.

Luke 5:4 (NKJV)

Do you need to take the courage to go out into the deep
in order to experience the touch of the Holy Spirit? With
God, everything is possible! Deep calls to deep. Cry out to
him in prayer today, and ask him to speak to you. Listen,
and then write it down.

_____

_____

_____

_____

_____

_____

_____

_____

_____

_____

_____

_____

> No one, having put his hand to the plow, and look-
> ing back, is fit for the kingdom of God.
>
> Luke 9:62 (NKJV)

Give no time to become depressed over what is gone. Never look back or listen to the enemy when he says, "All is lost," but press on, because much is to be gained in Jesus! He has a plan for you, and it is a good one. Ask him to reveal it to you today.

The weapons we fight with are not the weapons of the world. On the contrary, they have divine power to demolish strongholds.

2 Corinthians 10:4 (NIV)

As we fight and wrestle with certain strongholds in our lives, think about what your mind is struggling with. Our mind is the place where we fight with strongholds. Keep your mind renewed in the Word of God. Your hope and strength rest in the divine power Jesus gives us to fight the enemy. It is our mind and our thoughts he tries so hard to keep captive. In Christ, we are free.

_____

_____

_____

_____

_____

_____

_____

_____

_____

_____

_____

> Do not conform to the pattern of this world, but be transformed by the renewing of your mind. Then you will be able to test and approve what God's will is—his good, pleasing and perfect will.
>
> Romans 12:2 (NIV)

Do not allow the enemy to enter in to your mind and snatch away your ability to walk in the Fruit of the Spirit. Study your thoughts today. What are you thinking about the most. When you think of a negative thought, attack it in prayer and pray the opposite of what you are thinking. It will bring blessing and clear your mind.

But the fruit of the Spirit is love, joy, peace, forbearance, kindness, goodness, faithfulness

Galatians 5:22 (NKJV)

When we live by the voice of Gods spirit He will grant us all things. He is able to fill your heart with fruit that is sweet and tender. His mercies are new to you every morning. Gods love will fill you full which brings you to joy. His joy leads you to live in peace in all situations. Knowing His peace bestows forbearance and patience. When you guide your thoughts and steps with patience you reflect His goodness. When all these things flow from your life there is nothing left but your faithful heart for God. He will never give up on you. He loves you with an ever lasting love.

Choose to Love and all the fruits of the spirit will flow from you like living waters from heaven.

God Bless you.

Bibliography

The Bible Knowledge Commentary. John F. Walvoord, Roy B. Zuck. Colorado Springs: David C. Cook, 1983.

Dye,Michael, Patricia Fancher. *The Genesis Process.* 3rd ed. California: Genesis Addiction Process & Programs, 2003.